DEPARTMENT OF THE NAVY
HEADQUARTERS UNITED STATES MARINE CORPS
3000 MARINE CORPS PENTAGON
WASHINGTON, D.C. 20350-3000

FOOD SERVICE TRAINING AND READINESS MANUAL

DEPARTMENT OF THE NAVY
HEADQUARTERS UNITED STATES MARINE CORPS
3000 MARINE CORPS PENTAGON
WASHINGTON, D.C. 20350-3000

NAVMC 3500.35A
C 469
15 Jun 2010

NAVMC 3500.35A

From: Commandant of the Marine Corps
To: Distribution List

Subj: FOOD SERVICE TRAINING AND READINESS MANUAL, (SHORT TITLE: FOOD
       SERVICE T&R MANUAL)

Ref: (a) MCO P3500.72A
       (b) MCO 1553.3A
       (c) MCO 3400.3F
       (d) MCO 3500.27B W/Erratum
       (e) MCRP 3-0A
       (f) MCRP 3-0B
       (g) MCO 1553.2A

1. <u>Purpose</u>. Per reference (a), this T&R Manual establishes Core Capability
Mission Essential Tasks (MET) for readiness reporting and required events for
standardization training Marine Corps Food Service. Additionally, it
provides tasking for formal schools preparing personnel for service in the
Food Services Occupational Field. This NAVMC supersedes NAVMC 3500.35.

2. <u>Scope</u>

   a. The Core Capability Mission Essential Task List (METL) in this manual
is used in Defense Readiness Reporting System (DRRS) by all units for the
assessment and reporting of unit readiness. Units achieve training readiness
for reporting in DRRS by gaining and sustaining proficiency in the training
events in this manual at both collective (unit) and individual levels.

   b. Per reference (b), commanders will conduct an internal assessment of
the unit's ability to execute each MET, and develop long-, mid-, and short-
range training plans to sustain proficiency in each MET. Training plans will
incorporate these events to standardize training and provide objective
assessment of progress toward attaining combat readiness. Commanders will
keep records at the unit and individual levels to record training
achievements, identify training gaps, and document objective assessments of
readiness associated with training Marines. Commanders will use reference
(c) to incorporate nuclear, biological, and chemical defense training into
training plans and reference (d) to integrate operational risk management.
References (e) and (f) provide amplifying information for effective planning
and management of training within the unit.

c. Formal school and training detachment commanders will use references (a)
and (g) to ensure programs of instruction meet skill-training requirements
established in this manual, and provide career-progression training in the
events designated for initial training in the formal school environment.

DISTRIBUTION STATEMENT A: Approved for public release; distribution is
unlimited.

Management should be directed to: Commanding General, TECOM (Ground Training Branch C 469), 1019 Elliot Road, Quantico, VA 22134.

4. <u>Command</u>. This Directive is applicable to the Marine Corps Total Force.

5. <u>Certification</u>. Reviewed and approved this date.

M. DIGEPTESE
By direction

Distribution: PCN 10033197200

Copy to: 7000260 (2)
8145001 (1)

LOCATOR SHEET

Subj: FOOD SERVICE TRAINING AND READINESS MANUAL, (SHORT TITLE: FOOD
       SERVICE T&R MANUAL)

Location: _____
                (Indicate location(s) of copy(ies) of this Manual.)

RECORD OF CHANGES

Log completed change action as indicated.

Change Number	Date of Change	Date Entered	Signature of Person Incorporated Change

FOOD SERVICE T&R MANUAL

TABLE OF CONTENTS

CHAPTER

FOOD SERVICE T&R MANUAL

CHAPTER 1

OVERVIEW

FOOD SERVICE T&R MANUAL

CHAPTER 1

OVERVIEW

1000. INTRODUCTION

1. The T&R Program is the Corps' primary tool for planning, conducting and evaluating training, and assessing training readiness. Subject Matter Experts (SMEs) from the operating forces developed core capability Mission Essential Task Lists (METLs) for ground communities derived from the Marine Corps Task List (MCTL). T&R Manuals are built around these METLs and all events contained in T&R Manuals relate directly to this METL. This comprehensive T&R Program will help to ensure the Marine Corps continues to improve its combat readiness by training more efficiently and effectively. Ultimately, this will enhance the Marine Corps' ability to accomplish real-world missions.

2. The T&R Manual contains the individual and collective training requirements to prepare units to accomplish their combat mission. The T&R Manual is not intended to be an encyclopedia that contains every minute detail of how to accomplish training. Instead, it identifies the minimum standards that Marines must be able to perform in combat. The T&R Manual is a fundamental tool for commanders to build and maintain unit combat readiness. Using this tool, leaders can construct and execute an effective training plan that supports the unit's METL. More detailed information on the Marine Corps Ground T&R Program is found in reference (a).

1001. UNIT TRAINING

1. The training of Marines to perform as an integrated unit in combat lies at the heart of the T&R program. Unit and individual readiness are directly related. Individual training and the mastery of individual core skills serve as the building blocks for unit combat readiness. A Marine's ability to perform critical skills required in combat is essential. However, it is not necessary to have all individuals within a unit fully trained in order for that organization to accomplish its assigned tasks. Manpower shortfalls, temporary assignments, leave, or other factors outside the commander's control, often affect the ability to conduct individual training. During these periods, unit readiness is enhanced if emphasis is placed on the individual training of Marines on-hand. Subsequently, these Marines will be mission ready and capable of executing as part of a team when the full complement of personnel is available.

2. Commanders will ensure that all tactical training is focused on their combat mission. The T&R Manual is a tool to help develop the unit's training plan. In most cases, unit training should focus on achieving unit proficiency in the core capabilities METL. However, commanders will adjust their training focus to support METLs associated with a major OPLAN/CONPLAN or named operation as designated by their higher commander and reported accordingly in the Defense Readiness Reporting System (DRRS). Tactical

training will support the METL in use by the commander and be tailored to meet T&R standards. Commanders at all levels are responsible for effective combat training. The conduct of training in a professional manner consistent with Marine Corps standards cannot be over emphasized.

3. Commanders will provide personnel the opportunity to attend formal and operational level courses of instruction as required by this Manual. Attendance at all formal courses must enhance the warfighting capabilities of the unit as determined by the unit commander.

1002. UNIT TRAINING MANAGEMENT

1. Unit Training Management (UTM) is the application of the Systems Approach to Training (SAT) and the Marine Corps Training Principles. This is accomplished in a manner that maximizes training results and focuses the training priorities of the unit in preparation for the conduct of its wartime mission.

2. UTM techniques, described in references (b) and (e), provide commanders with the requisite tools and techniques to analyze, design, develop, implement, and evaluate the training of their unit. The Marine Corps Training Principles, explained in reference (b), provide sound and proven direction and are flexible enough to accommodate the demands of local conditions. These principles are not inclusive, nor do they guarantee success. They are guides that commanders can use to manage unit-training programs. The Marine Corps training principles are:

- Train as you fight
- Make commanders responsible for training
- Use standards-based training
- Use performance-oriented training
- Use mission-oriented training
- Train the MAGTF to fight as a combined arms team
- Train to sustain proficiency
- Train to challenge

3. To maintain an efficient and effective training program, leaders at every level must understand and implement UTM. Guidance for UTM and the process for establishing effective programs are contained in references (a) through (g).

1003. SUSTAINMENT AND EVALUATION OF TRAINING

1. The evaluation of training is necessary to properly prepare Marines for combat. Evaluations are either formal or informal, and performed by members of the unit (internal evaluation) or from an external command (external evaluation).

2. Marines are expected to maintain proficiency in the training events for their MOS at the appropriate grade or billet to which assigned. Leaders are responsible for recording the training achievements of their Marines. Whether it involves individual or collective training events, they must ensure proficiency is sustained by requiring retraining of each event at or

before expiration of the designated sustainment interval. Performance of the training event, however, is not sufficient to ensure combat readiness. Leaders at all levels must evaluate the performance of their Marines and the unit as they complete training events, and only record successful accomplishment of training based upon the evaluation. The goal of evaluation is to ensure that correct methods are employed to achieve the desired standard, or the Marines understand how they need to improve in order to attain the standard. Leaders must determine whether credit for completing a training event is recorded if the standard was not achieved. While successful accomplishment is desired, debriefing of errors can result in successful learning that will allow ethical recording of training event completion. Evaluation is a continuous process that is integral to training management and is conducted by leaders at every level and during all phases of planning and the conduct of training. To ensure training is efficient and effective, evaluation is an integral part of the training plan. Ultimately, leaders remain responsible for determining if the training was effective.

3. The purpose of formal and informal evaluation is to provide commanders with a process to determine a unit's/Marine's proficiency in the tasks that must be performed in combat. Informal evaluations are conducted during every training evolution. Formal evaluations are often scenario-based, focused on the unit's METs, based on collective training standards, and usually conducted during higher-level collective events. References (a) and (f) provide further guidance on the conduct of informal and formal evaluations using the Marine Corps Ground T&R Program.

1004. ORGANIZATION

1. T&R Manuals are organized in one of two methods: unit-based or community-based. Unit-based T&R Manuals are written to support a type of unit (Infantry, Artillery, Tanks, etc.) and contain both collective and individual training standards. Community-based are written to support an Occupational Field, a group of related Military Occupational Specialties (MOSs), or billets within an organization (EOD, NBC, Intel, etc.). T&R Manuals are comprised of chapters that contain unit METs, collective training standards (CTS), and individual training standards (ITS) for each MOS, billet, etc.

2. The Food Service T&R Manual is a community-based manual comprised of 4 chapters. Chapter 2 lists the Core Capability METs and the related E-Coded events that support them. Chapter 3 contains collective events. Chapters 4 through 6 contain individual events.

1005. T&R EVENT CODING

1. T&R events are coded for ease of reference. Each event has a 4-4-4-digit identifier. The first four digits are referred to as a "community" and represent the unit type or occupation (FDSV, 3302, 3372 and 3381). The second four digits represent the functional or duty area (ADMN, CTQA, EQMT, EXPD, etc.). The last four digits represent the level and sequence of the event.

2. The T&R levels are illustrated in Figure 1. An example of the T&R coding used in this Manual is shown in Figure 2.

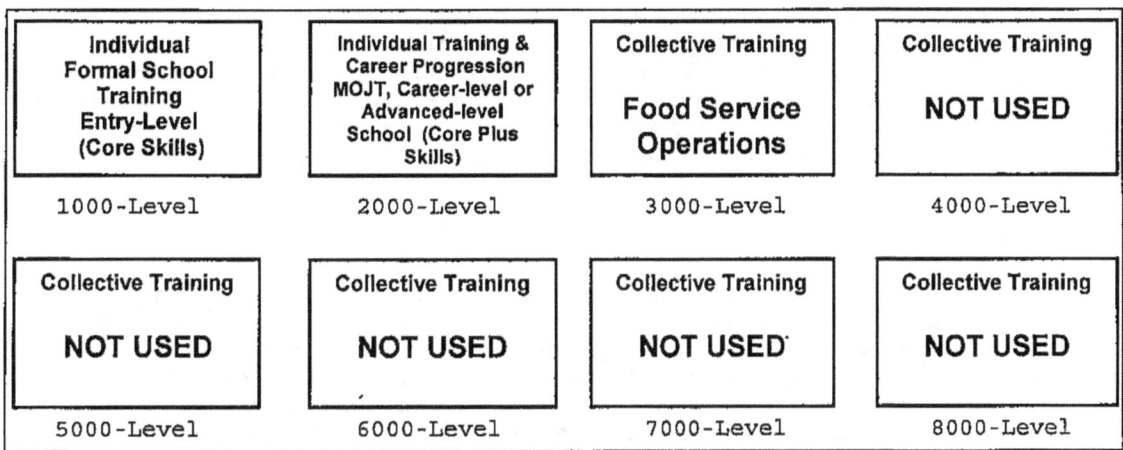

Figure 1:   T&R Event Levels

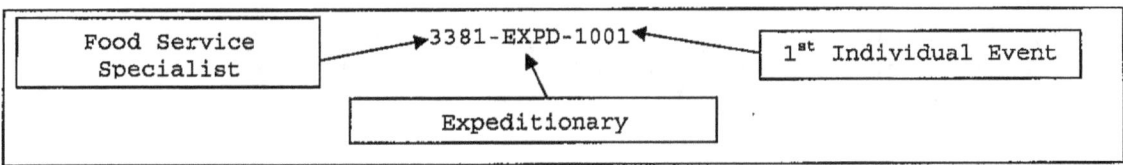

Figure 2:   T&R Event Coding

1006. COMBAT READINESS PERCENTAGE

1. The Marine Corps Ground T&R Program includes processes to assess readiness of units and individual Marines. Every unit in the Marine Corps maintains a basic level of readiness based on the training and experience of the Marines in the unit. Even units that never trained together are capable of accomplishing some portion of their missions. Combat readiness assessment does not associate a quantitative value for this baseline of readiness, but uses a "Combat Readiness Percentage", as a method to provide a concise descriptor of the recent training accomplishments of units and Marines.

2. Combat Readiness Percentage (CRP) is the percentage of required training events that a unit or Marine accomplishes within specified sustainment intervals.

3. In unit-based T&R Manuals, unit combat readiness is assessed as a percentage of the successfully completed and current (within sustainment interval) key training events called "Evaluation-Coded" (E-Coded) Events. E-Coded Events and unit CRP calculation are described in follow-on paragraphs. CRP achieved through the completion of E-Coded Events is directly relevant to readiness assessment in DRRS.

4. Individual combat readiness, in both unit-based and community-based T&R Manuals, is assessed as the percentage of required individual events in which a Marine is current. This translates as the percentage of training events for his/her MOS and grade (or billet) that the Marine successfully completes within the directed sustainment interval. Individual skills are developed through a combination of 1000-level training (entry-level formal school courses), individual on-the-job training in 2000-level events, and follow-on formal school training. Skill proficiency is maintained by retraining in each event per the specified sustainment interval.

1007. EVALUATION-CODED (E-CODED) EVENTS

1. Unit-type T&R Manuals can contain numerous unit events, some for the whole unit and others for integral parts that serve as building blocks for training. To simplify training management and readiness assessment, only collective events that are critical components of a mission essential task (MET), or key indicators of a unit's readiness, are used to generate CRP for a MET. These critical or key events are designated in the T&R Manual as Evaluation-Coded (E-Coded) events. Formal evaluation of unit performance in these events is recommended because of their value in assessing combat readiness. Only E-Coded events are used to calculate CRP for each MET.

2. The use of a METL-based training program allows the commander discretion in training. This makes the T&R Manual a training tool rather than a prescriptive checklist.

1008. CRP CALCULATION

1. Collective training begins at the 3000 level (team, crew or equivalent). Unit training plans are designed to accomplish the events that support the unit METL while simultaneously sustaining proficiency in individual core skills. Using the battalion-based (unit) model, the battalion (7000-level) has collective events that directly support a MET on the METL. These collective events are E-Coded and the only events that contribute to unit CRP. This is done to assist commanders in prioritizing the training toward the METL, taking into account resource, time, and personnel constraints.

2. Unit CRP increases after the completion of E-Coded events. The number of E-Coded events for the MET determines the value of each E-Coded event. For example, if there are 4 E-Coded events for a MET, each is worth 25% of MET CRP. MET CRP is calculated by adding the percentage of each completed and current (within sustainment interval) E-Coded training event. The percentage for each MET is calculated the same way and all are added together and divided by the number of METS to determine unit CRP. For ease of calculation, we will say that each MET has 4 E-Coded events, each contributing 25% towards the completion of the MET. If the unit has completed and is current on three of the four E-Coded events for a given MET, then they have completed 75% of the MET. The CRP for each MET is added together and divided by the number of METS to get unit CRP; unit CRP is the average of MET CRP.

For Example:

```
MET 1:  75% complete  (3 of 4 E-Coded events trained)
MET 2:  100% complete (6 of 6 E-Coded events trained)
MET 3:  25% complete  (1 of 4 E-Coded events trained)
MET 4:  50% complete  (2 of 4 E-Coded events trained)
MET 5:  75% complete  (3 of 4 E-Coded events trained)
```

To get unit CRP, simply add the CRP for each MET and divide by the number of METS:

MET CRP: 75 + 100 + 25 + 50 + 75 = 325

Unit CRP: 325 (total MET CRP)/ 5 (total number of METS) = 65%

1009. T&R EVENT COMPOSITION

1. This section explains each of the components of a T&R event. These items are included in all events in each T&R manual.

   a. <u>Event Code</u> (see Sect 1006). The event code is a 4-4-4 character set. For individual training events, the first 4 characters indicate the occupational function. The second 4 characters indicate functional area (TAC, CBTS, VOPS, etc.). The third 4 characters are simply a numerical designator for the event.

   b. <u>Event Title</u>. The event title is the name of the event.

   c. <u>E-Coded</u>. This is a "yes/no" category to indicate whether or not the event is E-Coded. If yes, the event contributes toward the CRP of the associated MET. The value of each E-Coded event is based on number of E-Coded events for that MET. Refer to paragraph 1008 for detailed explanation of E-Coded events.

   d. <u>Supported MET(s)</u>. List all METs that are supported by the training event.

   e. <u>Sustainment Interval</u>. This is the period, expressed in number of months, between evaluation or retraining requirements. Skills and capabilities acquired through the accomplishment of training events are refreshed at pre-determined intervals. It is essential that these intervals are adhered to in order to ensure Marines maintain proficiency.

   f. <u>Billet</u>. Individual training events may contain a list of billets within the community that are responsible for performing that event. This ensures that the billet's expected tasks are clearly articulated and a Marine's readiness to perform in that billet is measured.

   g. <u>Grade</u>. Each individual training event will list the rank(s) at which Marines are required to learn and sustain the training event.

   h. <u>Initial Training Setting</u>. For Individual T&R Events only, this specifies the location for initial instruction of the training event in one of three categories (formal school, managed on-the-job training, distance learning). Regardless of the specified Initial Training Setting, any T&R event may be introduced and evaluated during managed on-the-job training.

(1) "FORMAL" – When the Initial Training Setting of an event is identified as "FORMAL" (formal school), the appropriate formal school or training detachment is required to provide initial training in the event. Conversely, formal schools and training detachments are not authorized to provide training in events designated as Initial Training Setting "MOJT" or "DL." Since the duration of formal school training must be constrained to optimize Operating Forces' manning, this element provides the mechanism for Operating Forces' prioritization of training requirements for both entry-level (1000-level) and career-level (2000-level) T&R Events. For formal schools and training detachments, this element defines the requirements for content of courses.

(2) "DL" – Identifies the training event as a candidate for initial training via a Distance Learning product (correspondence course or MarineNet course).

(3) "MOJT" – Events specified for Managed On-the-Job Training are to be introduced to Marines, and evaluated, as part of training within a unit by supervisory personnel.

i. Event Description. Provide a description of the event purpose, objectives, goals, and requirements. It is a general description of an action requiring learned skills and knowledge (e.g. Camouflage the M1A1 Tank).

j. Condition. Describe the condition(s), under which tasks are performed. Conditions are based on a "real world" operational environment. They indicate what is provided (equipment, materials, manuals, aids, etc.), environmental constraints, conditions under which the task is performed, and any specific cues or indicators to which the performer must respond. When resources or safety requirements limit the conditions, this is stated.

k. Standard. The standard indicates the basis for judging effectiveness of the performance. It consists of a carefully worded statement that identifies the proficiency level expected when the task is performed. The standard provides the minimum acceptable performance parameters and is strictly adhered to. The standard for collective events is general, describing the desired end-state or purpose of the event. While the standard for individual events specifically describe to what proficiency level in terms of accuracy, speed, sequencing, quality of performance, adherence to procedural guidelines, etc., the event is accomplished.

l. Event Components. Describe the actions composing the event and help the user determine what must be accomplished and to properly plan for the event.

m. Prerequisite Events. Prerequisites are academic training or other T&R events that must be completed prior to attempting the task. They are lower-level events or tasks that give the individual/unit the skills required to accomplish the event. They can also be planning steps, administrative requirements, or specific parameters that build toward mission accomplishment.

n. <u>Chained Events</u>. Collective T&R events are supported by lower-level collective and individual T&R events. This enables unit leaders to effectively identify subordinate T&R events that ultimately support specific mission essential tasks. When the accomplishment of any upper-level events, by their nature, result in the performance of certain subordinate and related events, the events are "chained." The completion of chained events will update sustainment interval credit (and CRP for E-Coded events) for the related subordinate level events.

o. <u>Related Events</u>. Provide a list of all Individual Training Standards that support the event.

p. <u>References</u>. The training references are utilized to determine task performance steps, grading criteria, and ensure standardization of training procedures. They assist the trainee in satisfying the performance standards, or the trainer in evaluating the effectiveness of task completion. References are also important to the development of detailed training plans.

q. <u>Distance Learning Products</u> (IMI, CBT, MCI, etc.). Include this component when the event can be taught via one of these media methods vice attending a formal course of instruction or receiving MOJT.

r. <u>Support Requirements</u>. This is a list of the external and internal support the unit and Marines will need to complete the event. The list includes, but is not limited to:

- Range(s)/Training Area
- Ordnance
- Equipment
- Materials
- Other Units/Personnel
- Other Support Requirements

s. <u>Miscellaneous</u>. Provide any additional information that assists in the planning and execution of the event. Miscellaneous information may include, but is not limited to:

- Admin Instructions
- Special Personnel Certifications
- Equipment Operating Hours
- Road Miles

2. Community-based T&R manuals have several additional components not found in unit-based T&R manuals. These additions do not apply to this T&R Manual.

1010. **CBRNE TRAINING**

1. All personnel assigned to the operating force must be trained in chemical, biological, radiological, nuclear, and explosive incident defense (CBRNE), in order to survive and continue their mission in this environment. Individual proficiency standards are defined as survival and basic operating standards. Survival standards are those that the individual must master in order to survive CBRNE attacks. Basic operating standards are those that the

individual, and collectively the unit, must perform to continue operations in a CBRNE environment.

2.   In order to develop and maintain the ability to operate in an CBRNE environment, CBRNE training is an integral part of the training plan and events in this T&R Manual. Units should train under CBRNE conditions whenever possible. Per reference (c), all units must be capable of accomplishing their assigned mission in a contaminated environment.

1011. NIGHT TRAINING

1.   While it is understood that all personnel and units of the operating force are capable of performing their assigned mission in "every climate and place," current doctrine emphasizes the requirement to perform assigned missions at night and during periods of limited visibility. Basic skills are significantly more difficult when visibility is limited.

2.   To ensure units are capable of accomplishing their mission they must train under the conditions of limited visibility. Units should strive to conduct all events in this T&R Manual during both day and night/limited visibility conditions. When there is limited training time available, night training should take precedence over daylight training, contingent on individual, crew, and unit proficiency.

1012. OPERATIONAL RISK MANAGEMENT (ORM)

1.   ORM is a process that enables commanders to plan for and minimize risk while still accomplishing the mission. It is a decision making tool used by Marines at all levels to increase operational effectiveness by anticipating hazards and reducing the potential for loss, thereby increasing the probability of a successful mission. ORM minimizes risks to acceptable levels, commensurate with mission accomplishment.

2.   Commanders, leaders, maintainers, planners, and schedulers will integrate risk assessment in the decision-making process and implement hazard controls to reduce risk to acceptable levels. Applying the ORM process will reduce mishaps, lower costs, and provide for more efficient use of resources. ORM assists the commander in conserving lives and resources and avoiding unnecessary risk, making an informed decision to implement a course of action (COA), identifying feasible and effective control measures where specific measures do not exist, and providing reasonable alternatives for mission accomplishment. Most importantly, ORM assists the commander in determining the balance between training realism and unnecessary risks in training, the impact of training operations on the environment, and the adjustment of training plans to fit the level of proficiency and experience of Sailors/Marines and leaders. Further guidance for ORM is found in references (b) and (d).

1013. APPLICATION OF SIMULATION

1. Simulations/Simulators and other training devices shall be used when they are capable of effectively and economically supplementing training on the

identified training task. Particular emphasis shall be placed on simulators that provide training that might be limited by safety considerations or constraints on training space, time, or other resources. When deciding on simulation issues, the primary consideration shall be improving the quality of training and consequently the state of readiness. Potential savings in operating and support costs normally shall be an important secondary consideration.

2. Each training event contains information relating to the applicability of simulation. If simulator training applies to the event, then the applicable simulator(s) is/are listed in the "Simulation" section and the CRP for simulation training is given. This simulation training can either be used in place of live training, at the reduced CRP indicated; or can be used as a precursor training for the live event, i.e., weapons simulators, convoy trainers, observed fire trainers, etc. It is recommended that tasks be performed by simulation prior to being performed in a live-fire environment. However, in the case where simulation is used as a precursor for the live event, then the unit will receive credit for the live event CRP only. If a tactical situation develops that precludes performing the live event, the unit would then receive credit for the simulation CRP.

1014. MARINE CORPS GROUND T&R PROGRAM

1. The Marine Corps Ground T&R Program continues to evolve. The vision for Ground T&R Program is to publish a T&R Manual for every readiness-reporting unit so that core capability METs are clearly defined with supporting collective training standards, and to publish community-based T&R Manuals for all occupational fields whose personnel augment other units to increase their combat and/or logistic capabilities. The vision for this program includes plans to provide a Marine Corps training management information system that enables tracking of unit and individual training accomplishments by unit commanders and small unit leaders, automatically computing CRP for both units and individual Marines based upon MOS and rank (or billet). Linkage of T&R Events to the Marine Corps Task List (MCTL), through the core capability METs, has enabled objective assessment of training readiness in the DRRS.

2. DRRS measures and reports on the readiness of military forces and the supporting infrastructure to meet missions and goals assigned by the Secretary of Defense. With unit CRP based on the unit's training toward its METs, the CRP will provide a more accurate picture of a unit's readiness. This will give fidelity to future funding requests and factor into the allocation of resources. Additionally, the Ground T&R Program will help to ensure training remains focused on mission accomplishment and that training readiness reporting is tied to units' METLs.

FOOD SERVICE T&R MANUAL

CHAPTER 2

MISSION ESSENTIAL TASKS MATRIX

This chapter remains as a placeholder for future use.

FOOD SERVICE T&R MANUAL

CHAPTER 3

COLLECTIVE EVENTS

CHAPTER 3

COLLECTIVE EVENTS

3000. PURPOSE. This chapter contains all collective events for the Food Service community. A collective event is an event that an established unit would perform in combat. These events are linked to a Service-Level Mission Essential Task (MET). This linkage tailor's collective and individual training for the selected MET. Each collective event is composed of component events that provide the major actions required. This may be likely actions, list of functions, or procedures. Accomplishment and proficiency level required of component events are determined by the event standard.

3001. EVENT CODING. T&R events are coded for ease of reference. Each event has a 4-4-4 digit identifier. The first four digits represent the community or occupational field, "FDSV". The second four digits represent the functional or duty area (e.g. Administrative Functions (ADMN), Equipment (EQMT), etc.). The last four digits represent the level, and identifier number of the event. The Food Service collective events are only in the 3000 level. Every event has a unique identifier number from 001 to 999.

3002. INDEX OF COLLECTIVE EVENTS BY LEVEL

Event Code	E-Code	Event	Page
		3000-LEVEL EVENTS	
FDSV-CTQA-3001		Monitor Quality Control Program	3-4
FDSV-CTQA-3002		Conduct Technical Inspections	3-4
FDSV-EXPD-3101		Embark Equipment	3-4
FDSV-EXPD-3102		Establish an Expeditionary Feeding Site	3-5

3003. 3000-LEVEL EVENTS

FDSV-CTQA-3001: Monitor Quality Control Program

SUPPORTED MET(S): 2

EVALUATION-CODED: NO   SUSTAINMENT INTERVAL: 12 months

CONDITION: In a food service environment.

STANDARD: To ensure that operations outlined in the Quality Assurance
Surveillance Plan (QASP) meet specified standards.

EVENT COMPONENTS:
1. Inspect the quality of food preparation.
2. Review Statement of Work/SOP to determine requirements.
3. Perform Quality Assurance inspections according to evaluation schedules.
4. Report written findings.

REFERENCES:
1. MCO 10110.14 Marine Corps Food Service and Subsistence Program
2. MCRP 4-11-8A Marine Corps Field Feeding Program
3. NAVMED P-5010.1 Navy Preventive Medicine Manual
4. NAVMED P-5010.9 Ground Sanitation

FDSV-CTQA-3002: Conduct Technical Inspections

SUPPORTED MET(S): 2

EVALUATION-CODED: YES   SUSTAINMENT INTERVAL: 12 months

CONDITION: In a food service environment, given an inspection team,
publications, and evaluation checklists.

STANDARD: To ensure proper food preparation and correct use of personnel,
facilities, and equipment.

EVENT COMPONENTS:
1. Review evaluation results.
2. Publish results.

REFERENCES:
1. MCO 10110.14 Marine Corps Food Service and Subsistence Program
2. MCO P10110.34E U.S. Marine Corps Food Service and Subsistence Program
3. NAVMED P-5010.1 Navy Preventive Medicine Manual
4. NAVSUP P-421 Navy Food Service SOP

FDSV-EXPD-3101: Embark Equipment

SUPPORTED MET(S): 1

EVALUATION-CODED: YES   SUSTAINMENT INTERVAL: 12 months

CONDITION: In a field environment, given a units authorized Table of Equipment (T/E).

STANDARD: To ensure all appropriate equipment for operations is available, adequately accounted for, and secured.

EVENT COMPONENTS:
1. Gather personnel and equipment.
2. Load Equipment.
3. Review the referenced publications.
4. Review safety procedures.

REFERENCES:
1. TM 09211A-14 Tray Ration Heating System TM
2. TM 10-7360-204-13 Field Range (M-2) TM
3. TM 10757A-12 Food Transporter Parts List & Instructions
4. TM 4700 15H Marine Corps Ground Equip Record Procedures
5. ULSS 001302-15 User's Logistics Support Summary for Field Food Service System (FFSS)

FDSV-EXPD-3102: Establish an Expeditionary Feeding Site

SUPPORTED MET(S): 1

EVALUATION-CODED: YES   SUSTAINMENT INTERVAL: 12 months

CONDITION: In a field environment, given operational requirements and Unit Density List (UDL).

STANDARD: To ensure mission accomplishment.

EVENT COMPONENTS:
1. Identify location.
2. Establish Force Protection.
3. Employ equipment.
4. Employ logistical support as needed.
5. Prepare the Family of Field Feeding Rations and Enhancements.
6. Redeploy equipment.

REFERENCES:
1. TM 09211A-14 Tray Ration Heating System TM
2. TM 10-7360-204-13 Field Range (M-2) TM
3. TM 10757A-12 Food Transporter Parts List & Instructions
4. TM 4700 15H Marine Corps Ground Equip Record Procedures
5. TM 5-1080-200-13&P Operators' Organizational and Direct Support Manual for Lightweight Camouflage Screen Systems
6. ULSS 001302-15 User's Logistics Support Summary for Field Food Service System (FFSS)

FOOD SERVICE T&R MANUAL

CHAPTER 4

MOS 3302 INDIVIDUAL EVENTS

FOOD SERVICE T&R MANUAL

CHAPTER 4

MOS 3302 INDIVIDUAL EVENTS

4000. PURPOSE. This chapter details the individual events that pertain to the community. These events are linked to a service-level Mission Essential Tasks (MET). This linkage tailor's individual training for the selected MET. Each individual event provides an event title, along with the conditions events will be performed under, and the standard to which the event must be performed to be successful.

4001. ADMINISTRATIVE NOTES. T&R events are coded for ease of reference. Each event has a 4-4-4 digit identifier. The first four digits represent the occupational field or military occupational field (IOPS, or 9934). This chapter contains 9934 events. The second four digits represent the functional or duty area. The last four digits represent the level, and identifier number of the event. Every individual event has an identifier number from 001 to 999.

4002. INDEX OF INDIVIDUAL EVENTS

Event Code	Event	Page
	2000-LEVEL EVENTS	
3302-ADMN-2001	Develop Emergency/Catastrophe Feeding Plan	4-4
3302-ADMN-2002	Develop Food Service Appendix to Operation Order	4-4
3302-ADMN-2003	Manage Program Budgets	4-5
3302-ADMN-2004	Develop Standard Operating Procedures (SOP)	4-5
3302-ADMN-2005	Manage Safety Programs	4-6
3302-ADMN-2006	Prepare Naval Correspondence	4-6
3302-CTQA-2101	Perform Contracting Officer's Representative (COR) Duties	4-7
3302-EXPD-2201	Identify Food Service Logistical Requirements in Support of Garrison/Expeditionary Operations	4-8
3302-GARR-2301	Develop a Menu	4-8
3302-GARR-2302	Manage a Technical Inspection (TI)	4-9
3302-GARR-2303	Establish Mess Hall Facility Improvement Program Requirements	4-9
3302-SUBS-2401	Verify Financial Status Forms	4-10

4003. 2000-LEVEL EVENTS

3302-ADMN-2001: Develop Emergency/Catastrophe Feeding Plan

EVALUATION-CODED: NO   **SUSTAINMENT INTERVAL:** 12 months

MOS PERFORMING: 3302

GRADES: WO-1, CWO-2, CWO-3, CWO-4, CWO-5, CAPT, MAJ, LTCOL

INITIAL TRAINING SETTING: FORMAL

CONDITION: In a food service environment, given shelter sites, food preparation equipment, and subsistence.

STANDARD: To ensure implementation of emergency response can be executed within 24 hours.

PERFORMANCE STEPS:
1. Determine local feeding requirements.
2. Evaluate feeding capabilities.
3. Prepare the feeding plan
4. Staff plans to local operations department.
5. Implement upon order.

REFERENCES:
1. DOD 1338.10M DOD Food Service Manual
2. DSCP-HB 4155.2 Inspection of Operational Rations
3. JP 3-07.5 Joint Tactics, Techniques, and Procedures for Noncombatant Evacuation Operations
4. LEM Local Emergency Plans
5. MCO 10110.14 Marine Corps Food Service and Subsistence Program
6. MCRP 4-11-8A Marine Corps Field Feeding Program
7. MCRP 4-11.8A Food Service Reference Publication
8. NAVMED P-5010.1 Navy Preventive Medicine Manual
9. NAVMED P-5010.9 Ground Sanitation

3302-ADMN-2002: Develop Food Service Appendix to Operation Order

EVALUATION-CODED: NO   **SUSTAINMENT INTERVAL:** 12 months

MOS PERFORMING: 3302

GRADES: WO-1, CWO-2, CWO-3, CWO-4, CWO-5, CAPT, MAJ, LTCOL

INITIAL TRAINING SETTING: FORMAL

CONDITION: In a food service environment, given commander's intent, concept of operations, warning order, fragmentary order, and logistic requirements.

STANDARD: Ensure appropriate food service support.

PERFORMANCE STEPS:
1. Participate in operational planning team (OPT) meetings as required.
2. Verify the mission.
3. Verify the concept of operations.
4. Verify the overall concept and priorities of logistical support.
5. Analyze the situation, mission, execution, administration & logistics and the command & control.
6. Draft appropriate annex/appendix to the operation order.
7. Submit to appropriate authority.

REFERENCES:
1. MCO 10110.14 Marine Corps Food Service and Subsistence Program
2. MCRP 4-11-8A Marine Corps Field Feeding Program
3. MCWP 4-1 Logistics Operations
4. MCWP 4-11 Tactical Level Logistics

3302-ADMN-2003: Manage Program Budgets

EVALUATION-CODED: NO   **SUSTAINMENT INTERVAL:** 12 months

MOS PERFORMING: 3302

INITIAL TRAINING SETTING: FORMAL

CONDITION: In a food service environment, given administrative supplies and operational requirements.

STANDARD: To ensure that resources are allocated correctly.

PERFORMANCE STEPS:
1. Initiate budget process
2. Validate Food Preparation and Serving Equipment (FPSE) budget.
3. Validate Military Personnel Marine Corps (MPMC 1105) budget.
4. Validate Operations and Maintenance Marine Corps (O&MMC) budget.
5. Validate Whole Room Concept (WRC) budget.
6. Submit budgets.

REFERENCES:
1. DOD 1338.10M DOD Food Service Manual
2. DOD Financial Management Regulation (DoD FMR) 7000.14 Vol 2B Budget Formulation and Presentation (Chapters 4-19)
3. MCO 10110.14 Marine Corps Food Service and Subsistence Program

---

3302-ADMN-2004: Develop Standard Operating Procedures (SOP)

EVALUATION-CODED: NO   **SUSTAINMENT INTERVAL:** 12 months

MOS PERFORMING: 3302

GRADES: WO-1, CWO-2, CWO-3, CWO-4, CWO-5, CAPT, MAJ, LTCOL

INITIAL TRAINING SETTING: FORMAL

CONDITION: In a food service environment, given Orders and Directives, administrative supplies.

STANDARD: To ensure SOP is correctly formatted and contains all requirements.

PERFORMANCE STEPS:
1. Analyze requirements.
2. Identify specifications.
3. Submit for publication.

REFERENCES:
1. MCO 10110.14 Marine Corps Food Service and Subsistence Program
2. MCRP 4-11-8A Marine Corps Field Feeding Program

3302-ADMN-2005: Manage Safety Programs

EVALUATION-CODED: NO   **SUSTAINMENT INTERVAL**: 12 months

MOS PERFORMING: 3302

GRADES: WO-1, CWO-2, CWO-3, CWO-4, CWO-5, CAPT, MAJ, LTCOL

INITIAL TRAINING SETTING: MOJT

CONDITION: In a food service environment, given personnel and equipment.

STANDARD: To ensure compliance with published Orders and Directives.

PERFORMANCE STEPS:
1. Identify what PPE is required.
2. Provide appropriate PPE.
3. Develop ORM plan.
4. Implement ORM plan.
5. Provide sustainment training.
6. Document all training.

REFERENCES:
1. 29 CFR 1910.1200 Occupational Safety and Health Standards, Hazard Communication
2. MCO 3500.27B Operational Risk Management (ORM) (May 04)
3. MCO 5100.19_ W/CH 1-3 Marine Corps Traffic Safety Program (DRIVESAFE)
4. MCO 5100.29A Marine Corps Safety Program (Jul 04)
5. NAVMC 2692 Unit Safety Program Management Manual

3302-ADMN-2006: Prepare Naval Correspondence

EVALUATION-CODED: NO   **SUSTAINMENT INTERVAL**: 12 months

MOS PERFORMING: 3302

GRADES: WO-1, CWO-2, CWO-3, CWO-4, CWO-5, CAPT, MAJ, LTCOL

INITIAL TRAINING SETTING: MOJT

CONDITION: In a food service environment, given administrative supplies and computer assets.

STANDARD: Ensuring correspondence is developed and submitted without error.

PERFORMANCE STEPS:
1. Prepare endorsements.
2. Prepare multiple address letters.
3. Prepare memorandums.
4. Prepare point papers.
5. Prepare business letters.
6. Prepare email communications.
7. Perform office filing procedures.

REFERENCES:
1. MCO 5210.11E Marine Corps Records Management Program (Apr 06)
2. MCO P5600.31G Marine Corps Publications and Printing Regulations (Sep 93)
3. SECNAVINST 5216.5 Naval Correspondence Manual
4. SECNAVINST M-5210.2 Standard Subject Identification Code (SSIC) Manual

---

3302-CTQA-2101: Perform Contracting Officer's Representative (COR) Duties

EVALUATION-CODED: YES   SUSTAINMENT INTERVAL: 12 months

MOS PERFORMING: 3302

GRADES: WO-1, CWO-2, CWO-3, CWO-4, CWO-5, CAPT, MAJ, LTCOL

INITIAL TRAINING SETTING: FORMAL

CONDITION: In a food service environment, given contract requirements, administrative supplies, personnel, and computer assets.

STANDARD: To ensure contract compliance.

PERFORMANCE STEPS:
1. Validate Contract Deficiency Report
2. Submit final report to KO.
3. Provide sustainment training to ACOR

REFERENCES:
1. DFARS Defense Federal Acquisition Regulation Supplement
2. FAR Federal Acquisition Regulation
3. MCO 10110.14 Marine Corps Food Service and Subsistence Program
4. MCO 4200.29 Food Service Contracting

3302-EXPD-2201: Identify Food Service Logistical Requirements in Support of Garrison/Expeditionary Operations

EVALUATION-CODED: NO   **SUSTAINMENT INTERVAL:** 12 months

MOS PERFORMING: 3302

GRADES: WO-1, CWO-2, CWO-3, CWO-4, CWO-5, CAPT, MAJ, LTCOL

INITIAL TRAINING SETTING: FORMAL

CONDITION: Given a garrison or field feeding mission.

STANDARD: To ensure appropriate resources are available to facilitate mission accomplishment.

PERFORMANCE STEPS:
1. Establish Host Nation Support Agreement requirements.
2. Establish a Reciprocating Support Agreement.
3. Establish an expeditionary feeding site requirement.
4. Coordinate Maritime Pre-positioning Force assets.

REFERENCES:
1. MCO 10110.14 Marine Corps Food Service and Subsistence Program
2. MCRP 4-11-8A Marine Corps Field Feeding Program
3. MCWP 4-1 Logistics Operations

3302-GARR-2301: Develop a Menu

EVALUATION-CODED: NO   **SUSTAINMENT INTERVAL:** 12 months

MOS PERFORMING: 3302

GRADES: WO-1, CWO-2, CWO-3, CWO-4, CWO-5, CAPT, MAJ, LTCOL

INITIAL TRAINING SETTING: FORMAL

CONDITION: Given a garrison or field feeding mission.

STANDARD: To ensure that it is nutritionally balanced.

PERFORMANCE STEPS:
1. Determine patron nutritional needs.
2. Initiate menu planning board.
3. Create nutritional/educational awareness program
4. Coordinate with local dietitian.
5. Publish menu.

REFERENCES:
1. BUMEDINST 10110.6 Nutrition Standards and Education
2. MCO 10110.14 Marine Corps Food Service and Subsistence Program
3. MCO P10110.42B AFRS, April 1999

4. MCO P10110.43 Armed Forces Recipe Service Index of Recipes
5. NAVMEDINST 10110.1 Nutrition Allowance, Standards, and Education

---

3302-GARR-2302: Manage a Technical Inspection (TI)

EVALUATION-CODED: NO   **SUSTAINMENT INTERVAL**: 12 months

MOS PERFORMING: 3302

GRADES: WO-1, CWO-2, CWO-3, CWO-4, CWO-5, CAPT, MAJ, LTCOL

INITIAL TRAINING SETTING: FORMAL

CONDITION: In a food service environment.

STANDARD: To ensure sanitary food preparation and the efficient use of food service personnel, facilities and equipment.

PERFORMANCE STEPS:
1. Assign personnel to conduct the evaluation.
2. Apply Serv-safe principles.
3. Analyze the evaluation results.
4. Publish results.

REFERENCES:
1. MCO 10110.14 Marine Corps Food Service and Subsistence Program
2. NAVMED P-5010 Navy Sanitation
3. NAVMED P-5010.9 Ground Sanitation

3302-GARR-2303: Establish Mess Hall Facility Improvement Program Requirements

EVALUATION-CODED: NO   **SUSTAINMENT INTERVAL**: 12 months

MOS PERFORMING: 3302

GRADES: WO-1, CWO-2, CWO-3, CWO-4, CWO-5, CAPT, MAJ, LTCOL

INITIAL TRAINING SETTING:

CONDITION: In a food service environment.

STANDARD: To provide appropriate level food service facilities that meet mission requirements.

PERFORMANCE STEPS:
1. Determine requirements.
2. Submit to appropriate authority.

REFERENCES:
1. MCO 10110.14 Marine Corps Food Service and Subsistence Program
2. MCO P11000.7 Facilities Maintenance Management

3302-SUBS-2401: Verify Financial Status Forms

EVALUATION-CODED: YES   **SUSTAINMENT INTERVAL**: 12 months

MOS PERFORMING: 3302

GRADES: WO-1, CWO-2, CWO-3, CWO-4, CWO-5, CAPT, MAJ, LTCOL

INITIAL TRAINING SETTING: FORMAL

CONDITION: In a food service environment.

STANDARD: To ensure operation is maintained within established monetary limits.

PERFORMANCE STEPS:
1. Obtain required documents.
2. Review financial documents.
3. Submit documents.

REFERENCES:
1. MCO 10110.14 Marine Corps Food Service and Subsistence Program
2. MCRP 4-11-8A Marine Corps Field Feeding Program

CHAPTER 5

MOS 3372 INDIVIDUAL EVENTS

FOOD SERVICE T&R MANUAL

CHAPTER 5

MOS 3372 INDIVIDUAL EVENTS

5000. PURPOSE. This chapter details the individual events that pertain to the 3372, Marine Aide. These events are linked to a service-level Mission Essential Tasks (MET). This linkage tailor's individual training for the selected MET. Each individual event provides an event title, along with the conditions events will be performed under, and the standard to which the event must be performed to be successful.

5001. ADMINISTRATIVE NOTES. T&R events are coded for ease of reference. Each event has a 4-4-4 digit identifier. The first four digits represent the military occupational field (3372). The second four digits represent the functional or duty area. The last four digits represent the level, and identifier number of the event. Every individual event has an identifier number from 001 to 999.

5002. INDEX OF INDIVIDUAL EVENTS

5003. 2000-LEVEL EVENTS

3372-CUL-2001: Prepare a Gourmet Meal

EVALUATION-CODED: NO   SUSTAINMENT INTERVAL: 12 months

MOS PERFORMING: 3372

GRADES: CPL, SGT, SSGT, GYSGT, MSGT, MGYSGT

INITIAL TRAINING SETTING: FORMAL

CONDITION: In a General Officer Quarters, given the number of guests
attending, special dietary restrictions, a Budget, and recipes.

STANDARD: Ensuring the meal meets current five star industry standards.

PERFORMANCE STEPS:
1. Develop Menu.
2. Determine ingredient requirements.
3. Procure ingredients.
4. Prepare menu items.

REFERENCES:
1. Culinary Institute of America Professional Cooking
2. NAVMED P-5010.1 Navy Preventive Medicine Manual
3. Marine Aides Handbook

3372-CUL-2002: Serve a meal

EVALUATION-CODED: NO   SUSTAINMENT INTERVAL: 12 months

MOS PERFORMING: 3372

GRADES: CPL, SGT, SSGT, GYSGT, MSGT, MGYSGT

INITIAL TRAINING SETTING: FORMAL

CONDITION: In a General Officer's quarters, given a specific function and
appropriate tableware.

STANDARD: Ensuring the meal is served in accordance with proper etiquette,
the General officer's preferences and current industry standards.

PERFORMANCE STEPS:
1. Identify number of courses.
2. Identify type of service and sequence.
3. Plate and serve individual courses.
4. Clean up.

REFERENCES:
1. Starkey International Professional Household Management
2. Marine Aides Handbook

3372-CUL-2003: Prepare an off-site Executive Social Function

EVALUATION-CODED: NO   SUSTAINMENT INTERVAL: 12 months

MOS PERFORMING: 3372

GRADES: CPL, SGT, SSGT, GYSGT, MSGT, MGYSGT

INITIAL TRAINING SETTING: FORMAL

CONDITION: Given a remote location.

STANDARD: In accordance to the General's guidance.

PERFORMANCE STEPS:
1. Conduct site survey.
2. Develop menu.
3. Determine logistical support required.
4. Set up food prep and dinning areas.
5. Prepare food as required.
6. Serve the meal.
7. Clean offsite location.

REFERENCES:
1. Culinary Institute of America Professional Cooking
2. Starkey International Professional Household Management
3. Marine Aides Handbook

3372-CUL-2004: Coordinate a high volume social function

EVALUATION-CODED: NO   SUSTAINMENT INTERVAL: 12 months

MOS PERFORMING: 3372

GRADES: CPL, SGT, SSGT, GYSGT, MSGT, MGYSGT

INITIAL TRAINING SETTING: MOJT

CONDITION: Given a specified location.

STANDARD: Ensuring success of large social event in accordance with the General's guidance.

PERFORMANCE STEPS:
1. Determine type of event.
2. Coordinate support.
3. Supervise event.

4. Return site to high state of readiness.
5. Reconcile all records.

REFERENCES:
1. NAVMED P-5010.1 Navy Preventive Medicine Manual
2. Starkey International Professional Household Management
3. Marine Aides Handbook

3372-CUL-2005: Provide Bartending Service

EVALUATION-CODED: NO   SUSTAINMENT INTERVAL: 12 months

MOS PERFORMING: 3372

GRADES: CPL, SGT, SSGT, GYSGT, MSGT, MGYSGT

INITIAL TRAINING SETTING: FORMAL

CONDITION: Given an event, location, type of occasion, and appropriate bar accessories.

STANDARD: Ensuring appropriate amounts/type of spirits/beverages are readily available and served throughout the function.

PERFORMANCE STEPS:
1. Determine the number of guests attending.
2. Determine needed amounts of beverages, spirits and bar accessories.
3. Requisition items as required.
4. Set up beverage station.
5. Serve beverages.
6. Break down and clean up station.

REFERENCES:
1. Marine Aides Handbook

3372-HHM-2101: Prepare General Officer Uniforms

EVALUATION-CODED: NO   SUSTAINMENT INTERVAL: 12 months

MOS PERFORMING: 3372

GRADES: CPL, SGT, SSGT, GYSGT, MSGT, MGYSGT

INITIAL TRAINING SETTING: FORMAL

CONDITION: In a General Officer's quarters, given insignia, ribbons, medals, or badges.

STANDARD: Properly, in accordance with MCO P1020.34_ Marine Corps Uniform Regulations.

PERFORMANCE STEPS:
1. Identify the uniform.
2. Place devices, ribbons and insignia as appropriate.
3. Check for accuracy.
4. Place uniform in proper location.
5. Inform appropriate personnel.

REFERENCES:
1. MCO 1306.18 Standards for Marines Assigned to Duty as Enlisted Aide
2. MCO P1020.34G W/CH 1-4 Marine Corps Uniform Regulations

3372-HHM-2102: Prepare Official Civilian Attire for a General Officer

EVALUATION-CODED: NO   **SUSTAINMENT INTERVAL:** 12 months

MOS PERFORMING: 3372

GRADES: CPL, SGT, SSGT, GYSGT, MSGT, MGYSGT

INITIAL TRAINING SETTING: FORMAL

CONDITION: In a General Officer's quarters, given dress requirements.

STANDARD: Properly, in accordance with the General's guidance.

PERFORMANCE STEPS:
1. Determine the proper official attire.
2. Check for serviceability.
3. Press items as needed.
4. Place items for review.

REFERENCES:
1. MCO 1306.18 Standards for Marines Assigned to Duty as Enlisted Aide

---

3372-HHM-2103: Prepare Uniform and Civilian attire for a General Officer

EVALUATION-CODED: NO   **SUSTAINMENT INTERVAL:** 12 months

MOS PERFORMING: 3372

GRADES: CPL, SGT, SSGT, GYSGT, MSGT, MGYSGT

INITIAL TRAINING SETTING: FORMAL

CONDITION: In a travel status.

STANDARD: Properly, in accordance with the General's guidance.

PERFORMANCE STEPS:
1. Determine quantities to bring.
2. Pack luggage.

3. Ensure luggage is on transport.
4. Ensure luggage is removed from transport.
5. Press and have items available for travel duration.

REFERENCES:
1. MCO 1306.18 Standards for Marines Assigned to Duty as Enlisted Aide
2. MCO P1020.34G W/CH 1-4 Marine Corps Uniform Regulations

3372-HHM-2104: Provide Uniform/Clothing Maintenance

EVALUATION-CODED: NO   SUSTAINMENT INTERVAL: 12 months

MOS PERFORMING: 3372

GRADES: CPL, SGT, SSGT, GYSGT, MSGT, MGYSGT

INITIAL TRAINING SETTING: FORMAL

CONDITION: In a General Officer Quarters.

STANDARD: Properly, in accordance with the General's guidance and Marine Corps uniform regulations.

PERFORMANCE STEPS:
1. Identify items that require cleaning.
2. Remove all badges, insignia and devices.
3. Ensure pockets are empty.
4. Identify items that require tailoring or repair.
5. Clean and tailor as required.

REFERENCES:
1. MCO 1306.18 Standards for Marines Assigned to Duty as Enlisted Aide
2. MCO P1020.34G W/CH 1-4 Marine Corps Uniform Regulations

3372-HHM-2105: Prepare for an Executive Social Event

EVALUATION-CODED: NO   SUSTAINMENT INTERVAL: 12 months

MOS PERFORMING: 3372

GRADES: CPL, SGT, SSGT, GYSGT, MSGT, MGYSGT

INITIAL TRAINING SETTING: FORMAL

CONDITION: In a general officer's quarters, given a set function.

STANDARD: Ensuring success of the social event in accordance with the General's guidance.

PERFORMANCE STEPS:
1. Determine type of event.

2. Coordinate support.
3. Supervise event.
4. Return quarters to high state of readiness.
5. Reconcile all records.

REFERENCES:
1. NAVMED P-5010.1 Navy Preventive Medicine Manual
2. Starkey International Professional Household Management
3. Marine Aides Handbook

3372-HHM-2106: Provide Care for Official Guest

EVALUATION-CODED: NO   SUSTAINMENT INTERVAL: 12 months

MOS PERFORMING: 3372

GRADES: CPL, SGT, SSGT, GYSGT, MSGT, MGYSGT

INITIAL TRAINING SETTING: FORMAL

CONDITION: In a General Officers Quarters.

STANDARD: Ensure guests are cared for in accordance with the General's guidance.

PERFORMANCE STEPS:
1. Identify the guest.
2. Identify guest requirements.
3. Provide care.
4. Check for compliance.

REFERENCES:
1. Starkey International Professional Household Management
2. Marine Aides Handbook

3372-HHM-2107: Supervise Minor/Major Construction projects

EVALUATION-CODED: NO   SUSTAINMENT INTERVAL: 12 months

GRADES: CPL, SGT, SSGT, GYSGT, MSGT, MGYSGT

INITIAL TRAINING SETTING: FORMAL

CONDITION: In a General Officers Quarters.

STANDARD: Ensuring compliance with Base Housing regulations.

PERFORMANCE STEPS:
1. Identify construction requirements.
2. Coordinate construction with appropriate authorities.

3. Supervise work performed.
4. Coordinate Quality control with appropriate authorities

REFERENCES:
1. Starkey International Professional Household Management
2. Marine Aides Handbook

3372-HHM-2108: Process Mail

EVALUATION-CODED: NO   SUSTAINMENT INTERVAL: 12 months

MOS PERFORMING: 3372

GRADES: CPL, SGT, SSGT, GYSGT, MSGT, MGYSGT

INITIAL TRAINING SETTING: FORMAL

CONDITION: In a General Officer's quarters.

STANDARD: Ensuring all command postal policies are enforced.

PERFORMANCE STEPS:
1. Identify Mail requirements.
2. Distribute mail as required.
3. Reconcile with appropriate authority.

REFERENCES:
1. Marine Aides Handbook

3372-HHM-2109: Coordinate Maintenance

EVALUATION-CODED: NO   SUSTAINMENT INTERVAL: 12 months

MOS PERFORMING: 3372

GRADES: CPL, SGT, SSGT, GYSGT, MSGT, MGYSGT

INITIAL TRAINING SETTING: FORMAL

CONDITION: In a General Officer's quarters, given maintenance requirements beyond Marine Aide's capability.

STANDARD: Ensuring all property, appliances and equipment are in a high state of readiness.

PERFORMANCE STEPS:
1. Identify needed maintenance.
2. Review applicable warranties.
3. Call appropriate maintenance authority.
4. Supervise maintenance.
5. Finalize maintenance logs.

REFERENCES:
1. Marine Aides Handbook

3372-HHM-2110: Account for Personal Cash, Checks, and Credit Card Usage

EVALUATION-CODED: NO   **SUSTAINMENT INTERVAL:** 12 months

MOS PERFORMING: 3372

GRADES: CPL, SGT, SSGT, GYSGT, MSGT, MGYSGT

INITIAL TRAINING SETTING: FORMAL

CONDITION: In a General Officer's quarters, given personal funds.

STANDARD: Ensuring funds are properly utilized.

PERFORMANCE STEPS:
1. Develop Accounting log book/automated log.
2. Maintain receipts.
3. Reconcile as requested.

REFERENCES:
1. Marine Aides Handbook

3372-HHM-2111: Develop a Inter office Communications Plan

EVALUATION-CODED: NO   **SUSTAINMENT INTERVAL:** 12 months

MOS PERFORMING: 3372

GRADES: CPL, SGT, SSGT, GYSGT, MSGT, MGYSGT

INITIAL TRAINING SETTING: FORMAL

CONDITION: In a general officer's quarters, given a computer, telephone, VTC, and administrative supplies.

STANDARD: Ensuring the General, command staff and appropriate personnel are properly informed.

PERFORMANCE STEPS:
1. Gather required contact information.
2. Determine the most effective form of Communication.
3. Submit input into the household management binder.
4. Utilize effective communication.

REFERENCES:
1. Starkey International Professional Household Management
2. Marine Aides Handbook

3372-HHM-2112: Perform Executive Housekeeping

EVALUATION-CODED: NO   **SUSTAINMENT INTERVAL:** 12 months

MOS PERFORMING: 3372

GRADES: CPL, SGT, SSGT, GYSGT, MSGT, MGYSGT

INITIAL TRAINING SETTING: FORMAL

CONDITION: In a General Officers Quarters.

STANDARD: Ensuring the cleanliness of the quarters is in accordance with General's guidance.

PERFORMANCE STEPS:
1. Identify areas of responsibility.
2. Develop zones.
3. Assemble cleaning supplies.
4. Clean zones.

REFERENCES:
1. Starkey International Professional Household Management
2. Marine Aides Handbook

3372-HHM-2113: Supervise Grounds Care

EVALUATION-CODED: NO   **SUSTAINMENT INTERVAL:** 12 months

MOS PERFORMING: 3372

GRADES: CPL, SGT, SSGT, GYSGT, MSGT, MGYSGT

INITIAL TRAINING SETTING: FORMAL

CONDITION: In the General Officer Quarters, given landscaping contract.

STANDARD: Ensuring the performance of duties necessary to the upkeep and maintenance of assigned quarters.

PERFORMANCE STEPS:
1. Identify areas of responsibility.
2. Ensure grounds are in compliance with contract.
3. Inspect areas.
4. Identify discrepancies if applicable.
5. Perform after action review.

REFERENCES:
1. Starkey International Professional Household Management
2. Marine Aides Handbook

3372-HHM-2114: Develop Household Management Binder

EVALUATION-CODED: NO   **SUSTAINMENT INTERVAL:** 12 months

MOS PERFORMING: 3372

GRADES: CPL, SGT, SSGT, GYSGT, MSGT, MGYSGT

INITIAL TRAINING SETTING: FORMAL

CONDITION: In the General Officer Quarters, given administrative supplies, and office equipment.

STANDARD: Ensuring uniform actions of personnel events and tasks are accomplished.

PERFORMANCE STEPS:
1. Analyze requirements.
2. Draft standards/ procedures.
3. Staff standards/ procedures.
4. Publish operating procedures.
5. Inspect adherence to operating procedures.
6. Identify changes.
7. Publish changes.
8. Perform after action review.

REFERENCES:
1. Starkey International Professional Household Management
2. Marine Aides Handbook

3372-HHM-2115: Coordinate vendor support

EVALUATION-CODED: NO   **SUSTAINMENT INTERVAL:** 12 months

MOS PERFORMING: 3372

GRADES: CPL, SGT, SSGT, GYSGT, MSGT, MGYSGT

INITIAL TRAINING SETTING: FORMAL

CONDITION: Given a requirement and supporting organization.

STANDARD: Ensuring the General Officer quarters is maintained in a high state of readiness.

PERFORMANCE STEPS:
1. Identify appropriate vendor.
2. Set up site visit as required.
3. Schedule appointment.
4. Supervise task.
5. Inspect the work completed.
6. Finalize billing.

REFERENCES:
1. Starkey International Professional Household Management
2. Marine Aides Handbook

3372-HHM-2116: Account for General Officer Quarters assets

EVALUATION-CODED: NO   SUSTAINMENT INTERVAL: 12 months

MOS PERFORMING: 3372

GRADES: CPL, SGT, SSGT, GYSGT, MSGT, MGYSGT

INITIAL TRAINING SETTING: FORMAL

CONDITION: Given a requirement.

STANDARD: Ensuring 100% accountability of government furnished equipment.

PERFORMANCE STEPS:
1. Identify Government furnished property.
2. Identify Communication assets.
3. Develop equipment/property replacement plan.
4. Reconcile with appropriate authority.

REFERENCES:
1. Marine Aides Handbook

3372-HHM-2117: Utilize Official Government Credit Card

EVALUATION-CODED: NO   SUSTAINMENT INTERVAL: 12 months

MOS PERFORMING: 3372

GRADES: CPL, SGT, SSGT, GYSGT, MSGT, MGYSGT

INITIAL TRAINING SETTING: MOJT

CONDITION: Given a requirement.

STANDARD: Ensuring government funds are spent according to the Department of the Navy policies and procedures.

PERFORMANCE STEPS:
1. Identify the types of funds to be utilized.
2. Fill out forms.
3. Purchase items as required.
4. Reconcile with appropriate authority

REFERENCES:
1. Marine Aides Handbook

3372-HHM-2118: Supervise Social Functions

EVALUATION-CODED: NO   **SUSTAINMENT INTERVAL:** 12 months

MOS PERFORMING: 3372

GRADES: SGT, SSGT, GYSGT, MSGT, MGYSGT

INITIAL TRAINING SETTING: MOJT

CONDITION: Given a requirement and support personnel.

STANDARD: Ensuring the event is accomplished in accordance with the General Officers guidance.

PERFORMANCE STEPS:
1. Identify the event.
2. Identify the requirements.
3. Execute mission.
4. Perform after action review.

REFERENCES:
1. Marine Aides Handbook

3372-HHM-2119: Record Expenditures

EVALUATION-CODED: NO   **SUSTAINMENT INTERVAL:** 12 months

MOS PERFORMING: 3372

GRADES: CPL, SGT, SSGT, GYSGT, MSGT, MGYSGT

INITIAL TRAINING SETTING: MOJT

CONDITION: In a General Officer's quarters, given official functions receipts and an expenditure logbook.

STANDARD: Ensuring all official funds are properly accounted for.

PERFORMANCE STEPS:
1. Gather the receipts.
2. Total out receipts.
3. Record in expenditure logbook or automated log.
4. Turn records into appropriate authorities.

REFERENCES:
1. Marine Aides Handbook

3372-HHM-2120: Coordinate Ceremonial Flag arrangements

EVALUATION-CODED: NO   **SUSTAINMENT INTERVAL:** 12 months

MOS PERFORMING: 3372

GRADES: CPL, SGT, SSGT, GYSGT, MSGT, MGYSGT

INITIAL TRAINING SETTING: MOJT

CONDITION: In a General Officer's quarters, given an official function and appropriate flags.

STANDARD: Ensuring flags are positioned in accordance with Marine Corps regulations.

PERFORMANCE STEPS:
1. Identify the function.
2. Coordinate with appropriate authorities.
3. Supervise flag placement and removal

REFERENCES:
1. Marine Aides Handbook

FOOD SERVICE T&R MANUAL

CHAPTER 6

MOS 3381 INDIVIDUAL EVENTS

FOOD SERVICE T&R MANUAL

CHAPTER 6

MOS 3381 INDIVIDUAL EVENTS

6000. PURPOSE. This chapter details the individual events that pertain to MOS 3381, Food Service Specialist. These events are linked to a service-level Mission Essential Tasks (MET). This linkage tailor's individual training for the selected MET. Each individual event provides an event title, along with the conditions events will be performed under, and the standard to which the event must be performed to be successful.

6001. ADMINISTRATIVE NOTES. T&R events are coded for ease of reference. Each event has a 4-4-4 digit identifier. The first four digits represent the military occupational field (3381). The second four digits represent the functional or duty area. The last four digits represent the level, and identifier number of the event. Every individual event has an identifier number from 001 to 999.

6002. INDEX OF INDIVIDUAL EVENTS

3381-CTQA-2202	Conduct a Technical Inspection (TI) of a Food Service Facility	6-26
3381-CTQA-2203	Perform Assistant Contracting Officer Representative (ACOR) Duties	6-26
3381-CUR-2301	Perform Curator Duties	6-27
3381-EQMT-2401	Supervise Embarkation of Food Service Equipment	6-28
3381-EXPD-2501	Plan Expeditionary Food Service Operations	6-28
3381-EXPD-2502	Supervise Preventative Maintenance Checks and Services	6-29
3381-EXPD-2503	Supervise the operation of Field Food Service Equipment	6-29
3381-FDPR-2601	Prepare the Advance Preparation Worksheet	6-30
3381-GARR-2701	Establish Mess Hall Facility Improvement Program	6-30
3381-MAP-2801	Provide Executive Level Food Service Support	6-30

6003.   1000-LEVEL EVENTS

3381-ADMN-1001:   Prepare Product Sheets

EVALUATION-CODED: NO   SUSTAINMENT INTERVAL: 12 months

MOS PERFORMING: 3381

GRADES: PVT, PFC, LCPL

INITIAL TRAINING SETTING: FORMAL

CONDITION: In a food service environment, given administrative supplies, appropriate recipes and forms.

STANDARD: To ensure that all calculations are correct.

PERFORMANCE STEPS:
1.   Determine product to be prepared.
2.   Obtain correct recipe.
3.   Obtain appropriate administrative items.
4.   Perform calculations for each ingredient.
5.   Document all calculations.
6.   Obtain approval from authorized personnel.

REFERENCES:
1.   MCO 10110.14 Marine Corps Food Service and Subsistence Program
2.   MCO 10110.42C Armed Forces Recipe Service Cards
3.   MCO P10110.43 Armed Forces Recipe Service Index of Recipes

---

3381-EQMT-1101:   Prepare Field Food Service Equipment for Embarkation

EVALUATION-CODED: NO   SUSTAINMENT INTERVAL: 12 months

MOS PERFORMING: 3381

GRADES: PVT, PFC, LCPL

INITIAL TRAINING SETTING: MOJT

CONDITION: In a food service environment.

STANDARD: To ensure compliance with embarkation plan.

PERFORMANCE STEPS:
1.   Review publications.
2.   Identify required equipment.
3.   Place equipment/items into appropriate containers.
4.   Secure containers.
5.   Place appropriate markings on containers.

REFERENCES:
1. MCO 10110.14 Marine Corps Food Service and Subsistence Program
2. MCRP 4-11.8A Food Service Reference Publication
3. MCWP 4-1 Logistics Operations
4. TM 08955B QUADCON Supplement #1
5. TM 08955C_14_P QUADCON TM

3381-EXPD-1201: Operate Field Food Service Equipment

EVALUATION-CODED: NO   **SUSTAINMENT INTERVAL:** 12 months

MOS PERFORMING: 3381

GRADES: PVT, PFC, LCPL

INITIAL TRAINING SETTING: FORMAL

CONDITION: In a field environment.

STANDARD: To ensure food service support is provided while sustaining operational conditions.

PERFORMANCE STEPS:
1. Review the appropriate publication(s).
2. Gather equipment.
3. Perform operations safety check.
4. Operate equipment.

REFERENCES:
1. TM 09211A-14 Tray Ration Heating System TM
2. TM 10-7360-204-13 Field Range (M-2) TM
3. TM 10879A-12 Field Food Service System Technical Manual (Commercial)

3381-EXPD-1202: Perform Preventative Maintenance Checks and Services

EVALUATION-CODED: NO   **SUSTAINMENT INTERVAL:** 12 months

MOS PERFORMING: 3381

GRADES: PVT, PFC, LCPL

INITIAL TRAINING SETTING: FORMAL

CONDITION: In a food service environment, given equipment, equipment record jacket, appropriate tools and administrative supplies.

STANDARD: To ensure field food service equipment is always maintained in an operational state of readiness.

PERFORMANCE STEPS:
1. Open ERO.

2. Perform initial inspection.
3. Identify missing or broken components.
4. Document all work on ERO.
5. Order repair parts utilizing EROSL, if required.
6. Perform repairs, if required.
7. Evacuate equipment if repairs are beyond authorized level of maintenance.
8. Complete Product Quality Deficiency Report (SF 368) if required.
9. Complete repairs.
10. Close ERO.
11. Document all actions in Equipment Record Jacket.

REFERENCES:
1. MCO 5210.11E Marine Corps Records Management Program (Apr 06)
2. MCO P4790.2C MIMMS Field Procedures Manual (Jul 94)
3. TM 10879A-12 Field Food Service System Technical Manual (Commercial)

3381-FDPR-1301: Demonstrate Proper Sanitation Practices

EVALUATION-CODED: NO   SUSTAINMENT INTERVAL: 12 months

MOS PERFORMING: 3381

GRADES: PVT, PFC, LCPL, CPL, SGT

INITIAL TRAINING SETTING: FORMAL

CONDITION: In a food service environment.

STANDARD: According to the guidelines outlined in NAVMED P5010.1&9.

PERFORMANCE STEPS:
1. Perform proper hygiene techniques.
2. Perform proper equipment sanitation techniques.
3. Perform proper food safety and handling procedures.

REFERENCES:
1. MCO 10110.14 Marine Corps Food Service and Subsistence Program
2. NAVMED P-5010.1 Navy Preventive Medicine Manual
3. NAVMED P-5010.9 Ground Sanitation

3381-FDPR-1302: Utilize Armed Forces Recipe Card Service

EVALUATION-CODED: NO   SUSTAINMENT INTERVAL: 12 months

MOS PERFORMING: 3381

GRADES: PVT, PFC, LCPL

INITIAL TRAINING SETTING: FORMAL

CONDITION: In a food service environment.

STANDARD: To ensure all food items are prepared correctly.

PERFORMANCE STEPS:
1. Determine product to be prepared.
2. Obtain appropriate recipe card.
3. Assemble equipment.
4. Assemble ingredients.
5. Prepare product using appropriate production method.
6. Place product in appropriate serving dishes.

REFERENCES:
1. MCO 10110.14 Marine Corps Food Service and Subsistence Program
2. MCO 10110.42C Armed Forces Recipe Service Cards
3. MCO P10110.43 Armed Forces Recipe Service Index of Recipes
4. NAVMED P-5010.1 Navy Preventive Medicine Manual
5. NAVMED P-5010.9 Ground Sanitation

3381-FDPR-1303: Prepare Eggs to Order

EVALUATION-CODED: NO   SUSTAINMENT INTERVAL: 12 months

MOS PERFORMING: 3381

GRADES: PVT, PFC, LCPL

INITIAL TRAINING SETTING: FORMAL

CONDITION: Given a recipe card.

STANDARD: In accordance with the Armed Forces Recipe Service Cards.

PERFORMANCE STEPS:
1. Identify equipment.
2. Assemble ingredients.
3. Prepare products.

REFERENCES:
1. MCO 10110.14 Marine Corps Food Service and Subsistence Program
2. MCO 10110.42C Armed Forces Recipe Service Cards
3. MCO P10110.43 Armed Forces Recipe Service Index of Recipes
4. NAVMED P-5010.1 Navy Preventive Medicine Manual

3381-FDPR-1304: Prepare Desserts

EVALUATION-CODED: NO   SUSTAINMENT INTERVAL: 12 months

MOS PERFORMING: 3381

GRADES: PVT, PFC, LCPL

INITIAL TRAINING SETTING: FORMAL

CONDITION: Given a recipe card.

STANDARD: In accordance with the Armed Forces Recipe Service Cards.

PERFORMANCE STEPS:
1. Identify equipment.
2. Assemble ingredients.
3. Prepare products.

REFERENCES:
1. MCO 10110.14 Marine Corps Food Service and Subsistence Program
2. MCO 10110.42C Armed Forces Recipe Service Cards
3. MCO P10110.43 Armed Forces Recipe Service Index of Recipes
4. NAVMED P-5010.1 Navy Preventive Medicine Manual

3381-FDPR-1305: Prepare Meat/Poultry/Seafood

EVALUATION-CODED: NO   SUSTAINMENT INTERVAL: 12 months

MOS PERFORMING: 3381

GRADES: PVT, PFC, LCPL

INITIAL TRAINING SETTING: FORMAL

CONDITION: Given a recipe card.

STANDARD: In accordance with the Armed Forces Recipe Service Cards.

PERFORMANCE STEPS:
1. Identify equipment.
2. Assemble ingredients.
3. Prepare products.

REFERENCES:
1. MCO 10110.14 Marine Corps Food Service and Subsistence Program
2. MCO 10110.42C Armed Forces Recipe Service Cards
3. MCO P10110.43 Armed Forces Recipe Service Index of Recipes
4. NAVMED P-5010.1 Navy Preventive Medicine Manual

3381-FDPR-1306: Prepare Salads

EVALUATION-CODED: NO   SUSTAINMENT INTERVAL: 12 months

MOS PERFORMING: 3381

GRADES: PVT, PFC, LCPL

INITIAL TRAINING SETTING: FORMAL

CONDITION: Given a recipe card.

STANDARD: In accordance with the quantities and ingredients specified in the recipe.

PERFORMANCE STEPS:
1. Identify equipment.
2. Assemble ingredients.
3. Prepare products.

REFERENCES:
1. MCO 10110.14 Marine Corps Food Service and Subsistence Program
2. MCO 10110.42C Armed Forces Recipe Service Cards
3. MCO P10110.43 Armed Forces Recipe Service Index of Recipes
4. NAVMED P-5010.1 Navy Preventive Medicine Manual

3381-FDPR-1307: Prepare Soups/Sauces/Gravies

EVALUATION-CODED: NO   **SUSTAINMENT INTERVAL**: 12 months

MOS PERFORMING: 3381

GRADES: PVT, PFC, LCPL

INITIAL TRAINING SETTING: FORMAL

CONDITION: Given a recipe card.

STANDARD: In accordance with the quantities and ingredients specified in the recipe.

PERFORMANCE STEPS:
1. Identify equipment.
2. Assemble ingredients.
3. Prepare products.

REFERENCES:
1. MCO 10110.14 Marine Corps Food Service and Subsistence Program
2. MCO 10110.42C Armed Forces Recipe Service Cards
3. MCO P10110.43 Armed Forces Recipe Service Index of Recipes
4. NAVMED P-5010.1 Navy Preventive Medicine Manual

3381-FDPR-1308: Prepare Cereal/Pasta Products

EVALUATION-CODED: NO   **SUSTAINMENT INTERVAL**: 12 months

MOS PERFORMING: 3381

GRADES: PVT, PFC, LCPL

INITIAL TRAINING SETTING: FORMAL

CONDITION: Given a recipe card.

STANDARD: In accordance with the Armed Forces Recipe Service Cards.

PERFORMANCE STEPS:
1. Identify equipment.
2. Assemble ingredients.
3. Prepare products.

REFERENCES:
1. MCO 10110.14 Marine Corps Food Service and Subsistence Program
2. MCO 10110.42C Armed Forces Recipe Service Cards
3. MCO P10110.43 Armed Forces Recipe Service Index of Recipes
4. NAVMED P-5010.1 Navy Preventive Medicine Manual

3381-FDPR-1309: Prepare Beverages

EVALUATION-CODED: NO   SUSTAINMENT INTERVAL: 12 months

MOS PERFORMING: 3381

GRADES: PVT, PFC, LCPL

INITIAL TRAINING SETTING: FORMAL

CONDITION: Given a recipe card.

STANDARD: In accordance with the Armed Forces Recipe Service Cards.

PERFORMANCE STEPS:
1. Identify equipment.
2. Assemble ingredients.
3. Prepare products.

REFERENCES:
1. MCO 10110.14 Marine Corps Food Service and Subsistence Program
2. MCO 10110.42C Armed Forces Recipe Service Cards
3. MCO P10110.43 Armed Forces Recipe Service Index of Recipes
4. NAVMED P-5010.1 Navy Preventive Medicine Manual

3381-FDPR-1310: Prepare Vegetables

EVALUATION-CODED: NO   SUSTAINMENT INTERVAL: 12 months

MOS PERFORMING: 3381

GRADES: PVT, PFC, LCPL

INITIAL TRAINING SETTING: FORMAL

CONDITION: Given a recipe card.

STANDARD: In accordance with the Armed Forces Recipe Service Cards.

PERFORMANCE STEPS:
1. Identify equipment.
2. Assemble ingredients.
3. Prepare products.

REFERENCES:
1. MCO 10110.14 Marine Corps Food Service and Subsistence Program
2. MCO 10110.42C Armed Forces Recipe Service Cards
3. MCO P10110.43 Armed Forces Recipe Service Index of Recipes
4. NAVMED P-5010.1 Navy Preventive Medicine Manual

3381-FDPR-1311: Prepare Sandwiches

EVALUATION-CODED: NO   **SUSTAINMENT INTERVAL:** 12 months

MOS PERFORMING: 3381

GRADES: PVT, PFC, LCPL

INITIAL TRAINING SETTING: FORMAL

CONDITION: Given a recipe card.

STANDARD: In accordance with the Armed Forces Recipe Service Cards.

PERFORMANCE STEPS:
1. Identify equipment.
2. Assemble ingredients.
3. Prepare products.

REFERENCES:
1. MCO 10110.14 Marine Corps Food Service and Subsistence Program
2. MCO 10110.42C Armed Forces Recipe Service Cards
3. MCO P10110.43 Armed Forces Recipe Service Index of Recipes
4. NAVMED P-5010.1 Navy Preventive Medicine Manual

3381-FDPR-1312: Prepare Garnish

EVALUATION-CODED: NO   **SUSTAINMENT INTERVAL:** 12 months

MOS PERFORMING: 3381

GRADES: PVT, PFC, LCPL

INITIAL TRAINING SETTING: FORMAL

CONDITION: In a food service environment, given equipment and subsistence items.

STANDARD: Ensuring all food items include garnish that is fresh, appropriate for the dish and presents a pleasing presentation.

PERFORMANCE STEPS:
1. Identify equipment.
2. Assemble ingredients.
3. Prepare products.

REFERENCES:
1. MCI Course 334 Food Service Fundamentals
2. MCO 10110.14 Marine Corps Food Service and Subsistence Program
3. NAVMED P-5010.1 Navy Preventive Medicine Manual

3381-FDPR-1313: Prepare Pre-Cooked/Pre-Packaged Food Items

EVALUATION-CODED: NO   **SUSTAINMENT INTERVAL:** 12 months

MOS PERFORMING: 3381

GRADES: PVT, PFC, LCPL

INITIAL TRAINING SETTING: FORMAL

CONDITION: Given a recipe card.

STANDARD: In accordance with the manufacturer's instructions.

PERFORMANCE STEPS:
1. Identify equipment.
2. Assemble ingredients.
3. Prepare products.

REFERENCES:
1. MCO 10110.14 Marine Corps Food Service and Subsistence Program
2. MCO 10110.42C Armed Forces Recipe Service Cards
3. MCO P10110.43 Armed Forces Recipe Service Index of Recipes
4. NAVMED P-5010.1 Navy Preventive Medicine Manual

3381-GARR-1401: Operate Food Preparation and Service Equipment (FPSE)

EVALUATION-CODED: NO   **SUSTAINMENT INTERVAL:** 12 months

MOS PERFORMING: 3381

GRADES: PVT, PFC, LCPL

INITIAL TRAINING SETTING: FORMAL

CONDITION: In a food service environment.

STANDARD: To ensure all products are prepared in accurate quantities, acceptable quality within the prescribed time.

PERFORMANCE STEPS:
1. Perform preventive maintenance checks and services.
2. Clean and sanitize as required.

REFERENCES:
1. FPSE Manufacturers operating and safety instructions
2. NAVMED P-5010.1 Navy Preventive Medicine Manual

3381-GARR-1402: Perform Minor Property Functions

EVALUATION-CODED: NO   **SUSTAINMENT INTERVAL:** 12 months

MOS PERFORMING: 3381

GRADES: PVT, PFC, LCPL

INITIAL TRAINING SETTING: MOJT

CONDITION: In a food service environment.

STANDARD: To ensure government items are maintained and accounted for.

PERFORMANCE STEPS:
1. Maintain consumable supplies.
2. Perform inventory.

REFERENCES:
1. MCO 10110.14 Marine Corps Food Service and Subsistence Program
2. NAVMED P-5010.1 Navy Preventive Medicine Manual

3381-SUBS-1501: Perform Storeroom Functions

EVALUATION-CODED: NO   **SUSTAINMENT INTERVAL:** 12 months

MOS PERFORMING: 3381

GRADES: PVT, PFC, LCPL

INITIAL TRAINING SETTING: FORMAL

CONDITION: In a food service environment.

STANDARD: To ensure subsistence items are accounted for.

PERFORMANCE STEPS:
1. Receive subsistence items.
2. Issue subsistence items.
3. Perform inventory.
4. Rotate stock.
5. Perform housekeeping duties.

REFERENCES:
1. MCO 10110.14 Marine Corps Food Service and Subsistence Program
2. MCO P10110.34E U.S. Marine Corps Food Service and Subsistence Program
3. NAVMED P-5010.1 Navy Preventive Medicine Manual
4. NAVMED P-5010.9 Ground Sanitation

6004. 2000-LEVEL EVENTS

3381-ADMN-2001: Complete Cooks Worksheet/Menu

EVALUATION-CODED: NO   SUSTAINMENT INTERVAL: 12 months

MOS PERFORMING: 3381

GRADES: CPL, SGT

INITIAL TRAINING SETTING: FORMAL

CONDITION: In a food service environment, given administrative office equipment and food service requirements.

STANDARD: Ensuring accurate documentation of food items for each meal.

PERFORMANCE STEPS:
1. Prepare Cook's Worksheet.
2. Submit to Management.

REFERENCES:
1. MCO 10110.14 Marine Corps Food Service and Subsistence Program
2. MCO 10110.42C Armed Forces Recipe Service Cards
3. NAVMED P-5010.1 Navy Preventive Medicine Manual

3381-ADMN-2002: Validate the Financial Status

EVALUATION-CODED: NO   SUSTAINMENT INTERVAL: 12 months

MOS PERFORMING: 3381

GRADES: SSGT, GYSGT, MSGT, MGYSGT

INITIAL TRAINING SETTING: FORMAL

CONDITION: In a food service environment and given administrative equipment.

STANDARD: To ensure accuracy and financial solvency of a food service operation in relation to the target cost to feed.

PERFORMANCE STEPS:
1. Compare cost to feed of subsistence consumed to target cost.
2. Compare on-hand inventory level to authorized level.
3. Compare subsistence expenditures equating to under/over expenditure.

REFERENCES:
1. MCO 10110.14 Marine Corps Food Service and Subsistence Program

---

3381-ADMN-2003: Requisition Subsistence

EVALUATION-CODED: NO   **SUSTAINMENT INTERVAL:** 12 months

MOS PERFORMING: 3381

GRADES: SSGT, GYSGT

INITIAL TRAINING SETTING: FORMAL

CONDITION: In a food service environment and given administrative office equipment.

STANDARD: To ensure food items are available to support the Menu.

PERFORMANCE STEPS:
1. Review the requirements needed.
2. Verify the requirements.
3. Submit the requirements.

REFERENCES:
1. MCO 10110.14 Marine Corps Food Service and Subsistence Program
2. MCO 10110.42C Armed Forces Recipe Service Cards

3381-ADMN-2004: Coordinate Veterinarian Support

EVALUATION-CODED: NO   **SUSTAINMENT INTERVAL:** 12 months

MOS PERFORMING: 3381

GRADES: CPL, SGT, SSGT, GYSGT

INITIAL TRAINING SETTING: MOJT

CONDITION: In a food service environment, given damaged or deteriorated subsistence items.

STANDARD: To ensure all questionable food items are surveyed for wholesomeness and disposed of as directed.

PERFORMANCE STEPS:
1. Notify Veterinarian of damaged or deteriorated items.
2. Verify vets have inspected and taken samples of damaged or deteriorated items.
3. Await the outcome of results.
4. Conduct a survey of damaged or deteriorated food items.
5. Obtain and maintain proper documentation.

REFERENCES:
1. MCO 10110.21F Subsistence Inspection
2. MCO 10110.44 Veterinary/Medical Laboratory Food Safety and Quality Assurance Program
3. MCO P10110.31G Veterinary/Medical Food Inspection and Laboratory Service

4. NAVMED P-5010.1 Navy Preventive Medicine Manual
5. NAVMED P-5010.9 Ground Sanitation

3381-ADMN-2005: Submit Product Quality Deficiency Report

EVALUATION-CODED: NO   **SUSTAINMENT INTERVAL:** 12 months

MOS PERFORMING: 3381

GRADES: SSGT, GYSGT

INITIAL TRAINING SETTING: MOJT

CONDITION: In a food service office environment, given unsatisfactory material data, quality deficiency data on food service equipment, and forms.

STANDARD: To ensure unsatisfactory material is properly accounted for and disposed of appropriately.

PERFORMANCE STEPS:
1. Evaluate condition of subsistence/equipment to determine status.
2. Forward documents to higher headquarters.

REFERENCES:
1. MCO 10110:44 Veterinary/Medical Laboratory Food Safety and Quality Assurance Program
2. MCO P4200.15 Marine Corps Purchasing Procedures Manual - (obsolete MCO)

3381-ADMN-2006: Prepare Program Budgets

EVALUATION-CODED: NO   **SUSTAINMENT INTERVAL:** 12 months

GRADES: SSGT, GYSGT, MSGT, MGYSGT

INITIAL TRAINING SETTING: FORMAL

CONDITION: In a food service environment, given administrative supplies and operational requirements.

STANDARD: To ensure that resources are allocated correctly.

PERFORMANCE STEPS:
1. Complete Food Preparation and Serving Equipment (FPSE) budget.
2. Complete Operations and Maintenance Marine Corps (O&MMC) budget.
3. Complete Military Personnel Marine Corps (MPMC 1105) budget.
4. Complete Whole Room Concept (WRC) budget.
5. Submit budgets.

REFERENCES:
1. DOD 1338.10M DOD Food Service Manual

2. DOD Financial Management Regulation (DoD FMR) 7000.14 Vol 2B Budget Formulation and Presentation (Chapters 4-19)
3. MCO 10110.14 Marine Corps Food Service and Subsistence Program

---

3381-ADMN-2007: Establish Standard Operating Procedures (SOP)

EVALUATION-CODED: NO   **SUSTAINMENT INTERVAL:** 12 months

MOS PERFORMING: 3381

GRADES: SSGT, GYSGT, MSGT, MGYSGT

INITIAL TRAINING SETTING: MOJT

CONDITION: In a food service environment, given Orders and Directives, and administrative supplies.

STANDARD: To ensure uniform actions of subordinate personnel.

PERFORMANCE STEPS:
1. Analyze requirements.
2. Identify specifications.
3. Submit for publication.

REFERENCES:
1. MCO 10110.14 Marine Corps Food Service and Subsistence Program

---

3381-ADMN-2008: Manage Consolidated Memorandum Receipts (CMR)

EVALUATION-CODED: NO   **SUSTAINMENT INTERVAL:** 12 months

MOS PERFORMING: 3381

GRADES: SSGT, GYSGT

INITIAL TRAINING SETTING: FORMAL

CONDITION: In a food service environment, given a Table of Equipment (T/E), and administrative supplies.

STANDARD: To ensure accountability of all food service equipment.

PERFORMANCE STEPS:
1. Conduct inventory of equipment.
2. Reconcile inventory with current CMR.
3. Retain a copy of corrected CMR.

REFERENCES:
1. MCO 10110.14 Marine Corps Food Service and Subsistence Program
2. MCO P10150.1 Garrison Property [CMR] Policy Manual
3. UM 4400-124 FMF SASSY Using Unit Procedures

3381-ADMN-2009: Procure Equipment/Supplies

EVALUATION-CODED: NO   **SUSTAINMENT INTERVAL:** 12 months

MOS PERFORMING: 3381

GRADES: SSGT, GYSGT

INITIAL TRAINING SETTING: FORMAL

CONDITION: In a food service environment, given funds.

STANDARD: To ensure mission accomplishment.

PERFORMANCE STEPS:
1. Establish allowances.
2. Review allowances.
3. Determine equipment deficiencies.
4. Submit requisitions.
5. Ensure installation.

REFERENCES:
1. DOD Financial Management Regulation (DoD FMR) 7000.14 Vol 2B Budget Formulation and Presentation (Chapters 4-19)
2. FAR Federal Acquisition Regulation
3. MCRP 4-11.8A Food Service Reference Publication
4. NAVCOMPT Navy Comptroller Manual

3381-ADMN-2010: Perform Authorized Custodian/Cash Collection Agent Duties

EVALUATION-CODED: NO   **SUSTAINMENT INTERVAL:** 12 months

MOS PERFORMING: 3381

GRADES: CPL, SGT, SSGT, GYSGT

INITIAL TRAINING SETTING: FORMAL

CONDITION: In a food service environment, given a safe, cash box, NAVMC Forms 10298 and 10789, and appropriate administrative supplies.

STANDARD: To ensure proper safeguard of government funds from point of sale to turn-in.

PERFORMANCE STEPS:
1. Receive NAVMC Forms 10298 and 10789 from Cash Collection Agent.
2. Issue NAVMC Forms 10298 and 10789 to cashier.
3. Receive monies from cashier.
4. Turn-in monies to Cash Collection Agent.
5. Maintain records.

REFERENCES:
1. MCO 10110.14 Marine Corps Food Service and Subsistence Program

3381-ADMN-2011: Manage Automated Food Service Program

EVALUATION-CODED: NO   **SUSTAINMENT INTERVAL:** 12 months

MOS PERFORMING: 3381

GRADES: MSGT, MGYSGT

INITIAL TRAINING SETTING: FORMAL

CONDITION: In a food service environment, given an automated food management system, and appropriate forms.

STANDARD: To ensure information has been properly completed.

PERFORMANCE STEPS:
1. Forecast Subsistence Requirements.
2. Validate Subsistence Inventory.
3. Review Financial Commitments/Obligations.
4. Review Man-Day Fed Report.
5. Monitor Financial Status Report.
6. Retain documents.

REFERENCES:
1. MCO 10110.14 Marine Corps Food Service and Subsistence Program
2. MCO 10110.42C Armed Forces Recipe Service Cards
3. MCO P10110.35C Menu Standards

3381-ADMN-2012: Supervise Automated Food Service Program Operations

EVALUATION-CODED: NO   **SUSTAINMENT INTERVAL:** 12 months

MOS PERFORMING: 3381

GRADES: SSGT, GYSGT

INITIAL TRAINING SETTING: FORMAL

CONDITION: In a food service environment, given an automated food management system, and appropriate forms.

STANDARD: To ensure information has been properly completed.

PERFORMANCE STEPS:
1. Forecast Subsistence Requirements.
2. Verify Cooks Worksheet/Menu.
3. Verify Pull Sheets.
4. Verify Advance Preparation Worksheets.
5. Verify Subsistence Inventory.
6. Manage Purchase Orders.
7. Verify Subsistence Issue Receipts.
8. Verify Reconciliation of Bills.
9. Verify Man Day Fed Report.

10. Monitor Financial Status Report.
11. Retain documents.

REFERENCES:
1. MCO 10110.14 Marine Corps Food Service and Subsistence Program
2. MCO 10110.42C Armed Forces Recipe Service Cards
3. MCO P10110.35C Menu Standards

3381-ADMN-2013: Perform Automated Food Service Program Operations

EVALUATION-CODED: NO   SUSTAINMENT INTERVAL: 12 months

MOS PERFORMING: 3381

GRADES: CPL, SGT

INITIAL TRAINING SETTING: FORMAL

CONDITION: In a food service environment, given an automated food management system, and appropriate forms.

STANDARD: To ensure information has been properly completed.

PERFORMANCE STEPS:
1. Prepare Cooks Worksheet/Menu.
2. Prepare Pull Sheets.
3. Prepare Advance Preparation Worksheets.
4. Review Subsistence Inventory.
5. Requisition Subsistence.
6. Compile Subsistence Issue Receipts.
7. Reconciliation of Bills.
8. Maintain Man Day Fed Report.
9. Prepare Financial Status Report.
10. Retain documents.

REFERENCES:
1. MCO 10110.14 Marine Corps Food Service and Subsistence Program
2. MCO 10110.42C Armed Forces Recipe Service Cards
3. MCO P10110.35C Menu Standards

3381-ADMN-2014: Manage Equipment/Supplies

EVALUATION-CODED: NO   SUSTAINMENT INTERVAL: 12 months

MOS PERFORMING: 3381

GRADES: MSGT, MGYSGT

INITIAL TRAINING SETTING: MOJT

CONDITION: In a food service environment.

STANDARD: To ensure mission accomplishment.

PERFORMANCE STEPS:
1. Manage allowances.
2. Review equipment deficiencies.
3. Publish requisitions.

REFERENCES:
1. DOD Financial Management Regulation (DoD FMR) 7000.14 Vol 2B Budget
    Formulation and Presentation (Chapters 4-19)
2. FAR Federal Acquisition Regulation
3. MCRP 4-11-8A Marine Corps Field Feeding Program
4. NAVCOMPT Navy Comptroller Manual
5. UM 4790-5 Users Manual MIMMS

3381-ADMN-2015: Establish Food Service Appendix to Operation Order

EVALUATION-CODED: NO   SUSTAINMENT INTERVAL: 12 months

MOS PERFORMING: 3381

GRADES: MSGT, MGYSGT

INITIAL TRAINING SETTING: FORMAL

CONDITION: In a food service environment, given commander's intent, concept
of operations, warning order, fragmentary order, logistic requirements and
references.

STANDARD: To ensure there is a concept of support that meets mission specific
requirements as outlined in published references.

PERFORMANCE STEPS:
1. Participate in Operational Planning Team (OPT) meetings as required.
2. Draft appropriate annex/appendix to the operation order.
3. Submit to appropriate authority.

REFERENCES:
1. MCO 10110.14 Marine Corps Food Service and Subsistence Program
2. MCRP 4-11.8A Food Service Reference Publication
3. MCWP 4-1 Logistics Operations
4. MCWP 4-11 Tactical Level Logistics

3381-ADMN-2016: Manage Publication Control Program

EVALUATION-CODED: NO   SUSTAINMENT INTERVAL: 12 months

MOS PERFORMING: 3381

GRADES: CPL, SGT, SSGT, GYSGT

INITIAL TRAINING SETTING: MOJT

CONDITION: In a Food Service environment, given a unit T/O and unit T/E listing, and Publications Library Management System (PLMS) access.

STANDARD: To ensure required publications are maintained and updated as required.

PERFORMANCE STEPS:
1. Identify required publications by reviewing SL-1-2/SL-1-3.
2. Review publications library to assure that all publications and changes are required.
3. Request and validate publications that are required.
4. Implement changes as required.

REFERENCES:
1. MCO 10110.14 Marine Corps Food Service and Subsistence Program
2. PLMS Publications Library Management System
3. UM 4790-5 Users Manual MIMMS

3381-ADMN-2017: Develop Emergency/Catastrophe Feeding Plan

EVALUATION-CODED: NO   SUSTAINMENT INTERVAL: 12 months

MOS PERFORMING: 3381

GRADES: MSGT, MGYSGT

INITIAL TRAINING SETTING: FORMAL

CONDITION: In a food service environment, given shelter sites, food preparation equipment, subsistence and personnel.

STANDARD: To ensure implementation of emergency response can be executed within 24 hours.

PERFORMANCE STEPS:
1. Determine feeding requirements.
2. Evaluate feeding capabilities.
3. Prepare the feeding plan.
4. Execute upon order.

REFERENCES:
1. DOD 1338.10M DOD Food Service Manual
2. DSCP-HB 4155.2 Inspection of Operational Rations
3. JP 3-07.5 Joint Tactics, Techniques, and Procedures for Noncombatant Evacuation Operations
4. LEM Local Emergency Plans
5. MCO 10110.14 Marine Corps Food Service and Subsistence Program
6. MCRP 4-11-8A Marine Corps Field Feeding Program
7. NAVMED P-5010.1 Navy Preventive Medicine Manual
8. NAVMED P-5010.9 Ground Sanitation

3381-AIR-2101: Provide hospitality for Senior Executives

EVALUATION-CODED: NO   **SUSTAINMENT INTERVAL:** 12 months

MOS PERFORMING: 3381

BILLETS: Marine Aide Program

GRADES: GYSGT, MSGT, MGYSGT

INITIAL TRAINING SETTING: FORMAL

CONDITION: While in an executive mil-air flight status.

STANDARD: Ensuring all requirements are in accordance with the senior executive's guidance.

PERFORMANCE STEPS:
1. Identify VIP and requirements.
2. Develop plan.
3. Assemble needed ingredients and supplies.
4. Prepare meals.
5. Serve Meals.
6. Distribute comfort items.
7. Perform Flight crew duties.
8. Clean aircraft.
9. Conduct after action review.

REFERENCES:
1. Marine Aides Handbook

MISCELLANEOUS:

  ADMINISTRATIVE INSTRUCTIONS: In order to receive an assignment to the CMC plane, these Marines must attend the Air Crew Survival Training School-However this does not train them to do the tasks described above. Specific training provided by civilian education due to low volume of students per year.

3381-CTQA-2201: Perform Quality Assurance Evaluations

EVALUATION-CODED: NO   **SUSTAINMENT INTERVAL:** 12 months

MOS PERFORMING: 3381

GRADES: CPL, SGT

INITIAL TRAINING SETTING: FORMAL

CONDITION: In a food service environment, given required appropriate contracting documents.

STANDARD: To ensure that the contractor meets contract requirements.

PERFORMANCE STEPS:
1. Review required services of contract.
2. Conduct inspection.
3. Document findings.

REFERENCES:
1. MCO P10110.35C Menu Standards
2. MCRP 4-11-8A Marine Corps Field Feeding Program
3. NAVMED P-5010.1 Navy Preventive Medicine Manual
4. NAVMED P-5010.9 Ground Sanitation

3381-CTQA-2202: Conduct a Technical Inspection (TI) of a Food Service Facility

EVALUATION-CODED: NO   **SUSTAINMENT INTERVAL:** 12 months

MOS PERFORMING: 3381

GRADES: MSGT, MGYSGT

INITIAL TRAINING SETTING: FORMAL

CONDITION: In a food service environment.

STANDARD: Given required appropriate contracting documents.

PERFORMANCE STEPS:
1. Assign personnel to conduct the evaluation.
2. Apply Serv-safe principles.
3. Analyze the evaluation results.
4. Submit results.

REFERENCES:
1. MCO 10110.14 Marine Corps Food Service and Subsistence Program
2. NAVMED P-5010.1 Navy Preventive Medicine Manual
3. NAVMED P-5010.9 Ground Sanitation

3381-CTQA-2203: Perform Assistant Contracting Officer Representative (ACOR) Duties

EVALUATION-CODED: NO   **SUSTAINMENT INTERVAL:** 12 months

MOS PERFORMING: 3381

GRADES: SSGT, GYSGT

INITIAL TRAINING SETTING: FORMAL

CONDITION: In a food service environment, given contract requirements, and administrative supplies.

STANDARD: To ensure contract compliance.

PERFORMANCE STEPS:
1. Obtain contract requirements.
2. Develop inspection schedules.
3. Validate reports from Quality Assurance Evaluators (QAEs).
4. Submit to COR.
5. Maintain files.
6. Provide sustainment training to QAE's.

REFERENCES:
1. DFARS Defense Federal Acquisition Regulation Supplement
2. FAR Federal Acquisition Regulation
3. MCO 10110.14 Marine Corps Food Service and Subsistence Program
4. MCO 4200.29 Food Service Contracting
5. NAVCOMPT Navy Comptroller Manual
6. NAVMED P-5010.1 Navy Preventive Medicine Manual
7. NAVMED P-5010.9 Ground Sanitation
8. NAVSUP-486 Food Service Management General Messes

3381-CUR-2301: Perform Curator Duties

EVALUATION-CODED: NO   **SUSTAINMENT INTERVAL**: 12 months

MOS PERFORMING: 3381

BILLETS: Marine Aide Program

GRADES: SGT, SSGT, GYSGT, MSGT, MGYSGT

INITIAL TRAINING SETTING: FORMAL

CONDITION: In a General Officers Quarters.

STANDARD: Ensuring historical items are cared for according to industry standards.

PERFORMANCE STEPS:
1. Contact historical agencies.
2. Identify and record Historical items.
3. Clean and display items as required.

REFERENCES:
1. Starkey International Professional Household Management
2. Marine Aides Handbook

MISCELLANEOUS:

ADMINISTRATIVE INSTRUCTIONS: Specific training provided by civilian education due to low volume of students per year.

3381-EQMT-2401: Supervise Embarkation of Food Service Equipment

EVALUATION-CODED: NO   **SUSTAINMENT INTERVAL:** 12 months

MOS PERFORMING: 3381

GRADES: CPL, SGT

INITIAL TRAINING SETTING: MOJT

CONDITION: In a food service environment, given the required publications.

STANDARD: To ensure compliance with embarkation code.

PERFORMANCE STEPS:
1. Review publications.
2. Identify required equipment.
3. Submit documents.

REFERENCES:
1. MCO 10110.14 Marine Corps Food Service and Subsistence Program
2. MCRP 4-11-8A Marine Corps Field Feeding Program
3. MCWP 4-1 Logistics Operations
4. TM 08955B QUADCON Supplement #1
5. TM 08955C_14_P QUADCON TM

3381-EXPD-2501: Plan Expeditionary Food Service Operations

EVALUATION-CODED: NO   **SUSTAINMENT INTERVAL:** 12 months

MOS PERFORMING: 3381

GRADES: SSGT, GYSGT, MSGT, MGYSGT

INITIAL TRAINING SETTING: FORMAL

CONDITION: In a field environment.

STANDARD: To ensure food service support is provided while sustaining operational conditions.

PERFORMANCE STEPS:
1. Establish feed plan.
2. Conduct site survey, when applicable.
3. Execute Field Deployment/Planning checklist.
4. Determine external support requirements.
5. Submit requirements to appropriate agency.

REFERENCES:
1. MCO 10110.14 Marine Corps Food Service and Subsistence Program
2. MCRP 4-11.8A Food Service Reference Publication
3. MCWP 4-1 Logistics Operations

3381-EXPD-2502: Supervise Preventative Maintenance Checks and Services

EVALUATION-CODED: NO   SUSTAINMENT INTERVAL: 12 months

MOS PERFORMING: 3381

GRADES: CPL, SGT

INITIAL TRAINING SETTING: FORMAL

CONDITION: In a food service environment, given equipment, Equipment Record Jacket, appropriate tools and administrative supplies.

STANDARD: To ensure food service equipment is maintained in an operational state of readiness.

PERFORMANCE STEPS:
1. Supervise PMCS Schedule.
2. Reconcile ERO.
3. Reconcile EROSL.
4. File appropriate documentation.

REFERENCES:
1. MCO 5210.11E Marine Corps Records Management Program (Apr 06)
2. MCO P4790.1B Marine Corps Integrated Maintenance Management System Introduction
3. UM 4790-5 Users Manual MIMMS

3381-EXPD-2503: Supervise the operation of Field Food Service Equipment

EVALUATION-CODED: NO   SUSTAINMENT INTERVAL: 12 months

MOS PERFORMING: 3381

GRADES: CPL, SGT, SSGT, GYSGT

INITIAL TRAINING SETTING: FORMAL

CONDITION: In a field environment.

STANDARD: To ensure food service support is provided while sustaining operational conditions.

PERFORMANCE STEPS:
1. Review requirements.
2. Manage equipment operations.

REFERENCES:
1. MCO 10110.14 Marine Corps Food Service and Subsistence Program
2. MCRP 4-11-8A Marine Corps Field Feeding Program
3. TM 10879A-12 Field Food Service System Technical Manual (Commercial)

3381-FDPR-2601: Prepare the Advance Preparation Worksheet

EVALUATION-CODED: NO   **SUSTAINMENT INTERVAL:** 12 months

MOS PERFORMING: 3381

GRADES: CPL, SGT, SSGT, GYSGT

INITIAL TRAINING SETTING: FORMAL

CONDITION: In a food service environment.

STANDARD: To ensure adequate preparation of food items.

PERFORMANCE STEPS:
1. Review Production Worksheet.
2. Utilize the Armed Forces Recipe Service/Menu Scaled Recipes/Recipes to obtain requirements for advance preparation.
3. Prepare 72/48/24 hour Advance Preparation Worksheet.

REFERENCES:
1. MCO 10110.14 Marine Corps Food Service and Subsistence Program
2. MCO 10110.42C Armed Forces Recipe Service Cards
3. MCO P10110.35C Menu Standards
4. NAVMED P-5010.1 Navy Preventive Medicine Manual

3381-GARR-2701: Establish Mess Hall Facility Improvement Program

EVALUATION-CODED: NO   **SUSTAINMENT INTERVAL:** 12 months

MOS PERFORMING: 3381

GRADES: MSGT, MGYSGT

INITIAL TRAINING SETTING: FORMAL

CONDITION: In a food service environment.

STANDARD: To provide appropriate level food service facilities that meet mission requirements.

PERFORMANCE STEPS:
1. Identify requirements.
2. Forward to appropriate authority.

REFERENCES:
1. MCO 10110.14 Marine Corps Food Service and Subsistence Program

---

3381-MAP-2801: Provide Executive Level Food Service Support

EVALUATION-CODED: NO   **SUSTAINMENT INTERVAL:** 12 months

MOS PERFORMING: 3381

BILLETS: Marine Aide Program

GRADES: MSGT, MGYSGT

INITIAL TRAINING SETTING: FORMAL

CONDITION: Throughout the Marine corps, given a specific official requirement

STANDARD: Ensuring compliance with the General Officer's guidance.

PERFORMANCE STEPS:
1. Identify type of support.
2. Assign personnel.
3. Arrange travel.
4. Make liaison with event supervisor.
5. Perform necessary tasks.
6. Conduct after action review.

REFERENCES:
1. Marine Aides Handbook

MISCELLANEOUS:

 ADMINISTRATIVE INSTRUCTIONS: Specific training provided by civilian
 education due to low volume of students per year.

FOOD SERVICES T&R MANUAL

APPENDIX A

ACRONYMS AND ABBREVIATIONS

ADMN . . . . Administrative

AIR . . . . Air Crew

CTQA. . . . . .Contracting/QA

CUL . . . . .Culinary

CUR . . . . Curator

EQMT . . . . .Equipment Maintenance

EXPD . . . . .Expeditionary

FDPR. . . . . Food Production

GARR. . . . . .Garrison

HHM. . . . . Household Management

MAP. . . . . .Marine Aide Program

SUBS. . . . . Subsistence

FOOD SERVICE T&R MANUAL

APPENDIX B

REFERENCES

Department of Defense Directive (DODD)
DOD 1338.10M   Food Service Manual
DOD 7000.14   Financial Management Regulation (DoD FMR) Vol 2B Budget
                      Formulation and Presentation (Chapters 4-19)

Joint Publications (JPs)
JOINT PUB 3-07.2 Joint Tactics, Techniques, and Procedures for Antiterrorism

Secretary of the Navy Instructions
SECNAVINST 5216.5   Naval Correspondence Manual
SECNAVINST M-5210.2 Standard Subject Identification Code (SSIC) Manual

Marine Corps Orders
MCO 10110.14   Marine Corps Food Service and Subsistence Program
MCO 3500.27_   Operational Risk Management (ORM)
MCO 5100.29_   Marine Corps Safety Program
MCO 5210.11_   Marine Corps Records Management Program
MCO P5600.31_   Marine Corps Publications and Printing Regulations
MCO 4200.29   Food Service Contracting
MCO 10110.42C   Armed Forces Recipe Service Cards
MCO P10110.43   Armed Forces Recipe Service Index of Recipes
MCO P11000.7   Facilities Maintenance Management
P10110.34_   U.S. Marine Corps Food Service and Subsistence Program
MCO 1306.18   Standards for Marines Assigned to Duty as Enlisted Aide
MCO P1020.34_   Marine Corps Uniform Regulations W/CH 1-4
MCO P4790.2_   MIMMS Field Procedures Manual
MCO P10150.1   Garrison Property [CMR] Policy Manual
MCO P10110.35_   Menu Standards

Marine Corps Warfighting Publications (MCWPs)
MCWP 4-1   Logistics Operations

Marine Corps Reference Publications
MCRP 4-11-8A   Marine Corps Field Feeding Program

NAVMC Directives
NAVMC 2692   Unit Safety Program Management Manual

NAVMED Directives
NAVMED P-5010.1   Navy Preventive Medicine Manual
NAVMED P-5010.9   Ground Sanitation

NAVMEDINST
NAVMEDINST 10110.1 Nutrition Allowance, Standards, and Education

Technical Manuals
TM 08955B   QUADCON Supplement #1

TM 08955C_14_P   QUADCON TM
TM 09211A-14   Tray Ration Heating System TM
TM 10-7360-204-13 Field Range (M-2) TM
TM 10879A-12   Field Food Service System Technical Manual (Commercial)

Miscellaneous
LEM Local Emergency Plans

29 CFR 1910.1200 Occupational Safety and Health Standards, Hazard Communication

DFARS Defense Federal Acquisition Regulation Supplement

FAR Federal Acquisition Regulation

Culinary Institute of America Professional Cooking

Marine Aides Handbook

Starkey International Professional Household Management

FPSE Manufacturers operating and safety instructions

UM 4400-124 FMF SASSY Using Unit Procedures

NAVCOMPT Navy Comptroller Manual

PLMS Publications Library Management System

DSCP-HB 4155.2 Inspection of Operational Rations

NAVSUP-486 Food Service Management General Messes